VITAL
SIGNS
1993

VITAL SIGNS

1993

The Trends That Are Shaping Our Future

Lester R. Brown
Hal Kane
Ed Ayres

Editor: Linda Starke

with Derek Denniston
Alan Thein Durning
Christopher Flavin
Nicholas Lenssen
Sandra Postel
Michael Renner
David Malin Roodman
Linda Starke

W. W. Norton & Company

New York   London

Copyright © 1993 by Worldwatch Institute

The text of this book is composed in Garth Graphic with the
display set in Industria Alternate.
Composition and manufacturing by the Haddon Craftsmen, Inc.
Book design by Charlotte Staub.

ISBN 0–393–03517–4
ISBN 0–393–31024 8 (pbk)

W. W. Norton & Company, Inc.
500 Fifth Avenue, New York, N.Y. 10110
W. W. Norton & Company Ltd.
10 Coptic Street, London WC1A 1PU

2 3 4 5 6 7 8 9 0

 This book is printed on recycled paper

The collection of data appearing in *Vital Signs 1993* is available on 3.5 inch and 5.25 inch IBM-compatible diskettes for use with most spreadsheet software. To order the diskette pack, send check, money order, or credit card information (Visa or Master-Card) for $89.00 to Worldwatch Institute, 1776 Massachusetts Ave., NW, Washington, DC 20036 (telephone: 202-452-1999; fax: 202-296-7365).

CONTENTS

Part One: KEY INDICATORS

Part Two: SPECIAL FEATURES

ACKNOWLEDGMENTS

Compiling *Vital Signs* requires many people to generously share their data and knowledge. That information has come to Worldwatch in faxes, thick envelopes, and long phone conversations. We would like to thank all those who supplied it. Statisticians from the United Nations, government offices, public interest groups, universities, and corporations provided unpublished computer printouts, estimates, and projections based on the most current data, often with information broken down in unusual ways.

Here at Worldwatch, much of the information was adjusted, aggregrated, or restructured to become meaningful and coherent. We would like to thank Megan Ryan and Nancy Chege for their compilations of obscure data series. Perseverance and an extra helping hand during the galley stage came from Reah Janise Kauffman, executive assistant to the president.

Numerous people generously applied their expertise to reviews of specific topics; for that the various authors thank their colleagues at Worldwatch and Paul Gipe, Carl Haub, Norbert Henninger, Paul Maycock, Mack McFarland, Sten Nilsson, Ron Nowack, David Sweanor, and Helene Wilson. Independent editor Linda Starke, who ably handles all Worldwatch books, has also joined our authors' roster this time with two sections on population trends. The graphs—76 of them this year—were prepared in record time and with considerable patience about last-minute updates by Ross Feldner of New Age Graphics.

The *Vital Signs* series was launched last year with a startup grant from the Surdna Foundation. We sincerely thank the foundation, in particular executive director Edward Skloot, as well as Pete Myers and the W. Alton Jones Foundation for the importance they attach to disseminating information on key indicators, as evidenced by their ongoing project support.

General support for Worldwatch is provided by the Geraldine R. Dodge, William and Flora Hewlett, Andrew W. Mellon, Edward John Noble, Turner, and Frank Weeden foundations; by the Lynn R. and Karl E. Prickett and the Rockefeller Brothers funds; and by The Pew Charitable Trust. A personal grant for general support came from Roy Young. This project also benefited from information gathered and research done as part of projects supported by the Energy, Ford, George Gund, John D. and Catherine T. MacArthur, Charles Stewart Mott, Curtis and Edith Munson, and Public Welfare foundations.

For making a good idea better, by suggesting that we list the topics covered to date at the back of the book, special thanks go to Gordon Kane. And finally, we are indebted to the team of Iva Ashner and Andrew Marasia at W.W. Norton and Company for moving so quickly to get this volume into print.

Lester R. Brown
Hal Kane
Ed Ayres

FOREWORD

Sometimes new ideas work even better than expected. Such is the case with *Vital Signs*. Simple in concept, it is apparently responding to a widespread hunger for information on the trends that are reshaping our world. People do want to know what is happening to carbon emissions, to the fish catch, and to military expenditures.

This hunger for information is worldwide. In its first year, *Vital Signs* appeared in most of the world's major languages—Japanese, Chinese, German, French, Spanish, and Italian—in addition to English. The response has been enthusiastic, including reports from people who take the book with them on trips so they can draw on it when preparing for meetings or working on speeches. They simply won't leave home without it.

The design and content of this volume rest on the assumption that information is the key to intelligent action. My colleagues and I find *Vital Signs* invaluable in helping us shape our research program and establish priorities. Tracking the global trends it contains is helping us see things we have not seen before, thereby enriching the content and usefulness of our other publications. For example, as we analyzed the trends in *Vital Signs 1993*, we realized that growth in the oceanic fish catch had probably come to an end, thus closing an era of dependence on increases in the oceanic catch to expand the supply of seafood. In the new era, growth in fish supplies will come largely from expanding fish farming.

As we began updating the energy trends, it became clear that during the nineties the growth in wind generating capacity might well exceed that in nuclear generating capacity. As we analyzed trends in protein production, we began to see that the world is now facing difficulty in expanding all major sources of animal protein. Updating the bicycle and automobile production figures confirmed the bicycle's growing dominance as the world's leading vehicle for personal transportation. These few trends give a sense of the kind of information, insight, and surprises that *Vital Signs* provides.

Although we are pleased indeed to be able to publish this volume of key environmental trends, we regret that we cannot provide data for other important indicators, such as world losses of soil from erosion or the number of plant and animal extinctions each year. This volume, in a sense, provides an inventory of data availabilities and gaps.

Each year data on changes in world oil reserves are carefully compiled and published, for example, but we do not have a series on world soil reserves. Among major food-producing countries, only the United States regularly compiles data on topsoil losses from wind and water erosion. Civilization can survive the depletion of oil reserves, but it may not survive the continuing loss of topsoil at current rates.

On the food front, we know that grain consumption per person in Africa has been dropping for nearly two decades, but we do not know how much malnutrition has increased because there are no annual nutrition surveys. Only when malnutrition reaches its most severe stage—that of famine, which we can see on television—do we learn how extensive it is. Identifying and focusing attention on these information gaps is the first step to eventually eliminating them.

The Institute can produce this volume in part because over the last 19 years we have developed an extensive worldwide information-gathering network, one that permits us to assemble the trends in *Vital Signs* largely from data already in our files and data bases. Since we are actively researching these issues, we can also explain trends and give a sense of where they are heading, providing useful insights. It is this combination of information and insights that gives *Vital Signs* its value.

The structure of *Vital Signs 1993* is essentially the same as it was last year. Part One contains trends for which historical global data are available, such as the world grain harvest, coal production, and paper production. Each is presented in two pages, one with text and the other with data and graphs. Part Two contains essays on trends that are obviously important but for which no global historical data exist. Topics falling in this category include spreading water scarcity, declining marine mammal populations, and forest damage from acid rain.

A core group of indicators will appear in each volume, including trends such as meat production, nuclear power generation, and Third World debt. Other measures will appear from time to time, but not in every issue. This category, accounting for perhaps a third of the total, are typically trends that change very slowly.

In response to requests following publication of *Vital Signs 1992*, we are offering the data in *Vital Signs 1993* on disk. Included are not only the numbers appearing in the tables but also the data used to plot secondary graphs. We hope that by providing the information in this form, it will be even more widely used. Contact Gloria Grant at the Institute for details on how to order the disk.

The release of *Vital Signs 1992* generated more front-page news coverage than anything

the Institute has ever published. A number of newspapers and magazines not only reported on the trends in *Vital Signs*, they reprinted many of the graphs. Some have done this in clusters; others have done it serially. The *Los Angeles Times* devoted two thirds of a page to reprinting close to a dozen of the key indicators, including production of chlorofluorocarbons, bicycle production, the fish catch, and the global nuclear arsenal. As part of a news story, the *Chicago Tribune* reprinted several graphs, including those on world grain stocks, population, military expenditures, and the nuclear arsenal.

Touring Club Italiano, a half-million-member club headquartered in Milan, is carrying one indicator, including text, in each issue of its monthly magazine. And the *Guardian* in London frequently carries one of the key graphs in its "Friday Environment" section.

In summary, *Vital Signs* has been a valuable addition to our stable of publications, which consists of the Worldwatch Papers, *State of the World*, *World Watch* magazine, and the Environmental Alert book series. It is enormously expanding the flow of environmental information from the Institute, helping to raise environmental awareness throughout the world. We hope that more and more concerned people will be tracking the trends that are shaping the world in which we and our children will live.

We appreciate your notes indicating what you find useful in *Vital Signs* as well as suggested improvements. Some of the suggestions received over the past year have been incorporated in *Vital Signs 1993*. Keep your ideas coming and we will consider them as we work on *Vital Signs 1994*.

Lester R. Brown
May 1993

Worldwatch Institute
1776 Massachusetts Ave., N.W.
Washington, D.C. 20036

VITAL
SIGNS
1993

OVERVIEW
An Age of Discontinuity

Lester R. Brown

When the history of the late twentieth century is written, the nineties may well be seen as a decade of massive discontinuity. Long-established global trends that had been rising for decades—such as the seafood catch per person, growth in the nuclear arsenal, the production of chlorofluorocarbons (CFCs), coal use, and cigarette smoking rates—are now falling. Others that were going nowhere, or at best rising slowly, are suddenly soaring: the generation of electricity from wind, the use of compact fluorescent bulbs, and reliance on U.N. forces to keep peace, to name just three.

These trend reversals and the ones likely to follow could dwarf the discontinuities that occurred during the seventies in the wake of the 1973 rise in oil prices. At that time, an overnight tripling of oil prices boosted energy prices across the board, slowed the growth in automobile production, accelerated that of bicycles, and spurred investment in energy-efficient technologies, creating a new industry. As the shift from a buyer's market to a seller's market became a reality—spelling the end of cheap energy—world economic growth slowed, and it has never regained the rates prevailing before 1973. The oil price hike triggered the rise in Third World debt that eventually brought many developing economies to

their knees. The second oil price hike, in 1979, only reinforced those trends.

The discontinuities in the nineties stem not from rising energy prices but from spreading environmental degradation, new environmental constraints, and escalating environmental concerns. Production of CFCs, a major product of the world chemical industry, has been halved since 1988 because governments decided to save the stratospheric ozone layer that protects life on earth from damaging ultraviolet radiation. Similarly, a desire to stabilize climate and lower air pollution is leading governments to begin to discourage the use of fossil fuels. The conversion from a throwaway economy to a reuse/recycle one is now accelerating as efforts to reduce air pollution, acid rain, and carbon emissions gain momentum.

Constraints imposed by nature are also now directly affecting global economic trends. Among these are the capacity of crops to use fertilizer, of the oceans to yield seafood, and of the hydrological cycle to produce fresh water. In addition to a wholesale alteration of trends, these new environmental constraints and concerns are raising new challenges for political leaders.

A survey of the 42 global indicators compiled for this year's *Vital Signs* shows four new

---

Units of measure throughout this book are metric unless common usage dictates otherwise. Historical world population data used in per capita calculations are from the Center for International Research at the U.S. Bureau of the Census as of March 25, 1993.

challenges facing policymakers: First, it is becoming more difficult to expand the output of basic foodstuffs, such as grain, seafood, and livestock products, as fast as population. Second, the global economy is not expanding as easily as it once did. Third, we appear to be on the edge of a basic restructuring of the world energy economy. And fourth, the prospect that continuing rapid population growth could undermine living standards is becoming a reality.

THE NEW CHALLENGES

In the production of food, neither the world's farmers nor its fishing fleets are keeping pace with the growth in human numbers. Grain output per person has fallen 8 percent from the historical high reached in 1984, dropping roughly 1 percent a year. (See pp. 26–27.) There are no new technologies in prospect suggesting that farmers can restore the 3-percent annual rate of growth in the world grain harvest that prevailed from 1950 through 1984, helping to reduce hunger and malnutrition.

Expanding the world fish catch is even more difficult. The oceans may not be able to sustain a catch of more than 100 million tons, the level reached in 1989. With the take actually declining slightly since then, the catch per person has fallen 7 percent. (See pp. 32–33.) Meat production per person peaked one year later and then dropped nearly 1 percent over the next two years. (See pp. 30–31.)

Evidence is accumulating in the nineties that the world economy is not growing as easily as it once did. The 1990–92 global economic recession that launched the decade is at least as severe as those induced by oil price hikes in 1973–75 and 1980–82. During the 1990–92 period, the gross world product (GWP) per person—the sum of all goods and services produced—fell nearly 3 percent. (See pp. 72–73.) Even using GWP, an indicator that overstates progress because it omits environmental degradation and the depletion of natural capital, living conditions are deteriorating for much of humanity.

The conventional economic wisdom concerning the recession of the early nineties attributes it to economic mismanagement in ad-

vanced industrial countries, importantly the United States, Germany, and Japan, and to the disruption associated with economic reform in centrally planned economies. Though clearly major contributors, these are not the only forces slowing world economic growth. Growth in the fishing industry, which supplies a large share of the world's protein, may have ended. Growth in rangeland production of beef, mutton, and other livestock products (as contrasted with feedlot production) may also be close to an end. The world grain harvest continues to increase, but only at 1 percent per year since 1984, compared with 3 percent annually during the three preceding decades. Scarcities of fresh water are also limiting economic expansion in many countries. (See pp. 106–07.) With constraints emerging in these primary economic sectors—sectors on which much of the Third World depends—the world may be moving into an era of slower economic growth.

With the world energy economy, there are abundant signs that a major restructuring is imminent. On the broadest level, the restructuring is away from investment in fossil fuels and nuclear power and toward investment in efficiency and renewables. Among fossil fuels, the historical high in oil output occurred in 1979, and that of coal in 1989. (See pp. 46–47 and 56–57.) Use of natural gas, widely seen as providing the logical transition from a fossil-fuel-based economy to a solar/hydrogen one, is continuing to rise.

Nuclear power, once thought to be the energy source of the future, has failed to live up to its promise and is being challenged on economic grounds in most of the countries where it is produced. After continuing without interruption since the mid-fifties, growth in nuclear power came to a halt in 1990. (See pp. 50–51.)

Use of solar energy sources—from solar-thermal power plants and photovoltaic cells to wind energy—is on the rise. Recent advances in technologies, along with economic incentives adopted in the United States and Europe, may make wind power the first of the new generation of energy technologies to enter a period of massive growth.

Installed wind power capacity is expected to

grow rapidly in the United States and Europe, where several governments have launched ambitious wind power development programs. (See pp. 48–49.) During the nineties, growth in the world's wind-generating capacity is likely to exceed that of its nuclear-generating capacity.

Just as technological advances are brightening the future for renewable energy resources, so they are also leading to striking gains in energy efficiency—in light bulbs, electric motors, the thermal efficiency of windows, and cogenerating technologies that produce both electricity and heat.

New compact fluorescent bulbs are replacing incandescents, for example, providing the same amount of light but using only one fourth as much electricity. The 134 million compact fluorescents sold worldwide in 1992 save enough electricity to close 10 nuclear power plants. (See pp. 62–63.)

Perhaps the most disturbing trend challenging policymakers is the steady growth in population. The progress in slowing human population growth so evident in the seventies has stalled—with disturbing implications for the long-term trajectory of population growth. (See pp. 124–25.) Throughout the sixties and seventies, declining fertility held out hope for getting the brakes on population growth before it began to undermine living standards. The eighties, however, turned out to be a lost decade, one in which the United States not only abdicated its leadership role, it also withdrew all financial support from the U.N. Population Fund and the International Planned Parenthood Federation. This deprived millions of couples in the Third World of access to the family planning services needed to control the number or timing of their children.

Our generation is the first to witness the doubling of world population during a lifetime. Indeed, everyone born before 1950 has seen world population double. The annual increment has climbed throughout this century from 13 million in 1900 to 37 million in 1950 and to 91 million in 1992. (See pp. 94–95.)

One of the most immediate consequences of continuing rapid population growth is declines in the per capita grain harvest and fish catch.

For these two basic food sources, the needs of the 91 million being added each year can be satisfied only by reducing consumption of those already here. In effect, the world has moved into a new era—one that raises difficult questions about how resources are distributed between those here now and those who are just arriving.

The absence of any technology to reestablish the rapid growth in food production that existed from 1950 to 1984 is a matter of deepening concern. In early 1992, the U.S. National Academy of Sciences and the Royal Society of London together issued a report recognizing this new reality. In their words, "If current predictions of population growth prove accurate and patterns of human activity on the planet remain unchanged, science and technology may not be able to prevent either irreversible degradation of the environment or continued poverty for much of the world."[1]

Later that same year the Union of Concerned Scientists issued a statement signed by nearly 1,600 of the world's leading scientists, including 96 Nobel Prize recipients. They, too, expressed serious concern about the future, noting that the continuation of destructive human activities "may so alter the living world that it will be unable to sustain life in the manner that we know. . . . A great change in our stewardship of the earth and the life on it is required, if vast human misery is to be avoided and our global home on this planet is not to be irretrievably mutilated."[2]

Some of the issues emerging in the new age of discontinuity can be seen more clearly by looking at various combinations of the 42 indicators in this year's *Vital Signs*. The dramatic shift in the world protein economy, for example, can be seen in the parallel trends for seafood, meat, and soybeans as the per capita supply of each levels off or declines. The inability of the world's farmers to continue substituting fertilizer for land in many countries shows why the growth in food output has slowed so dramatically. Several trends—the production of fossil fuels, automobiles, and bicycles— show the broad dimensions of the energy transformation now beginning. And the successful use of taxes to discourage smoking offers hope that tax policy can be an important tool for reversing a range of destructive trends.

PROTEIN SHORTAGES EMERGING

As the nineties unfold, evidence of protein scarcity is accumulating in the production trends of three major sources of high-quality protein: seafood, meat, and soybeans. Between 1950 and 1989, the world fish catch expanded from 22 million to 100 million tons. Far outstripping growth in population, this more than doubled the seafood availability per person— from 9 to 19 kilograms. (See Figure 1.)

Throughout our lifetimes, the growing global demand for seafood has been satisfied by expanding the oceanic catch, but this era has now ended. Marine biologists at the U.N. Food and Agriculture Organization estimate that the 1989 catch of 100 million tons is the maximum yield that can be sustained by oceanic fisheries. Since then, the fish catch has actually declined slightly, bringing per capita seafood supplies from 19.4 kilograms in 1988 to 17.8 kilograms in 1992, a drop of more than 7 percent in three years. (See pp. 32–33.)

The other major natural system supplying protein is the earth's rangelands, which provide most of the feed for the world's cattle, sheep, and goat populations. But there is little remaining potential for further expanding

meat production through grazing. Indeed, in Africa, the Middle East, and much of Asia, rangelands are being widely overused, leading to the gradual destruction of this productive resource base.

The problems of expanding meat produced from grazing have slowed the growth in total meat production. From 1950 to 1990, world meat production increased nearly fourfold, with the annual growth being one of the most predictable trends in the world economy. (See pp. 30–31.) In per capita terms, meat production increased from 18.0 kilograms in 1950 to 32.3 kilograms in 1990, a rise of 79 percent over 40 years. During this period, meat output grew at nearly twice the rate of population. Between 1990 and 1992, however, it declined nearly 1 percent.

One of the keys to expanding both meat and fish production is the supply of soybean meal. An increase in fish supplies now depends on fish farming, and expanding meat output means either putting more cattle and sheep into feedlots or shifting from beef and mutton to pork or poultry—all of which depend on grain and soybean meal.

But growth in world soybean output has slowed dramatically over the last decade. From 1950 to 1979, the soybean harvest increased fivefold, expanding some 6 percent per year. (See pp. 28–29.) Soybean output per person tripled between 1950 and 1979 as it went from 7 kilograms to 21 kilograms. Since then, it has not increased at all.

In summary, the seafood catch per person is likely to decline as long as population continues to grow, leading to worsening scarcity. For meat produced from rangelands, prospects are similar. With substantial increases in protein supplies now depending on the use of ever-growing quantities of grain and soybeans, those who consume livestock products and fish are competing directly with those who need grain for food. In such a situation, the likelihood of spreading protein shortages increases.

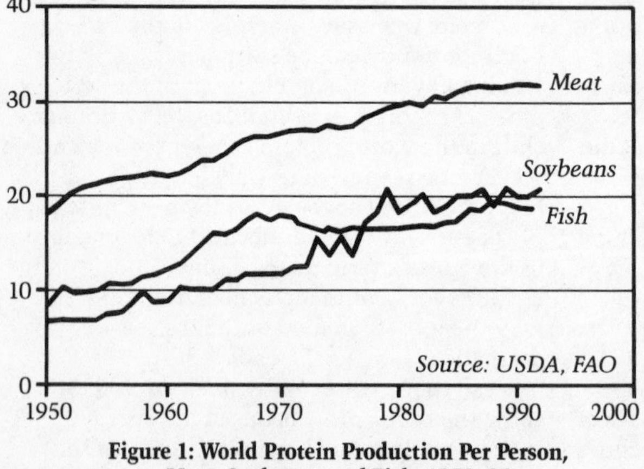

Figure 1: World Protein Production Per Person, Meat, Soybeans, and Fish, 1950–92

THE FERTILIZER CONSTRAINT

With little new land to bring under the plow, the world's farmers expand output largely by raising land productivity. This, in turn, has depended on using ever growing quantities of fertilizer.

In effect, farmers have increasingly substituted fertilizer for land in their efforts to keep up with the growth in world demand for food. (See Figure 2.) Since 1950, the harvested area of grain has increased by one quarter, while fertilizer use has increased tenfold, from 14 million tons to 140 million tons. In per capita terms, the grain harvested area per person has been nearly cut in half. (See pp. 40–41.) Fertilizer use, meanwhile, went from 5.5 kilograms per person in 1950 to a high of 28 kilograms in 1989, a fivefold increase over 39 years. (See pp. 42–43.)

Since 1989, however, world fertilizer use has declined in absolute terms, reducing per capita use from 28 kilograms to 23.9 kilograms, a drop of 15 percent. Growth in fertilizer use has come to a halt in Western Europe and the United States. U.S. fertilizer use in the early nineties is actually somewhat lower than in the early eighties, partly because farmers are matching fertilizer applications more precisely to crop needs.

In the former Soviet Union, fertilizer use dropped by half between 1988 and 1992. For the most part, this decline simply represents elimination of the wasteful use that existed prior to the 1988 economic reforms, which allowed fertilizer prices to rise to world market levels. It contrasts sharply with the situation in China, where fertilizer use increased threefold following the agricultural reforms initiated there in 1978.

The increasing use of fertilizer has been the principal engine of growth in the world food economy since 1950. With the potential for large further gains now diminishing, agricultural scientists are experiencing difficulty in

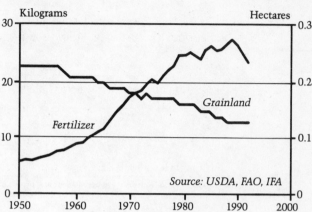

Figure 2: World Fertilizer and Grainland Per Person, 1950–92

developing technologies that will reestablish rapid growth in world food output.

ENERGY TRANSITION ACCELERATES

The key indicator for measuring progress in stabilizing climate is the carbon efficiency of the world economy—the value of goods and services produced per unit of carbon emitted. From 1950 to 1979, carbon efficiency increased little. After the second oil price hike, it increased much more rapidly, as overall energy efficiency climbed, raising economic output per kilogram of carbon emitted from $2.67 in 1979 to $3.19 in 1991. (See pp. 60–61.)

A second contributor to the rise in carbon efficiency is nuclear power. Between 1979 and 1990, the world added 214,000 megawatts of nuclear generating capacity, displacing large amounts of coal and oil. (See pp. 50–51.) The third source has been the substitution of natural gas for coal and oil over the last decade. Natural gas not only emits much less carbon per unit of energy produced than either oil or coal, it also burns cleaner, producing little air pollution or acid rain. All indications are that the growth in natural gas use during the nineties will continue at a pace much like that in the eighties.

The historical growth in oil production came to an end in 1979. (See pp. 46–47 and Table 1.)

19

TABLE 1. GROWTH AND DECLINE IN
PRODUCTION OF FOSSIL FUELS, 1950–92

	GROWTH PERIOD		DECLINE PERIOD	
FOSSIL FUEL	YEARS	ANNUAL RATE (percent)	YEARS	ANNUAL RATE (percent)
Oil	1950–79	+ 6.4	1979–92	− 0.5
Coal	1950–89	+ 2.2	1989–92	− 0.6
Natural Gas	1950–92	+ 6.2		

SOURCE: For oil and coal, see pages 46–47 and 56–57; natural gas from American
Petroleum Institute and Worldwatch Institute estimate based on British Petroleum.

For coal, the reversal came in 1989, as mounting environmental concerns led to its gradual replacement with natural gas in many countries. (See pp. 56–57.) While the decline in coal output since 1989 is too brief to be seen as a new long-term trend, it seems unlikely that coal burning will ever rise much above the level reached then.

For oil, the reversal in consumption was, initially at least, economic in origin—a response to higher prices. For coal, in contrast, the reversal is environmental in origin—a response to rising concern about the effects of air pollution on human health, of acid rain on forest productivity, and of global warming on the economy.

In the future, anticipated gains in the overall efficiency of energy use will continue to increase the carbon efficiency of the world economy. Sales of compact fluorescent bulbs, for example, have increased some 36 percent a year during the last five years. (See pp. 62–63.) This is but one of the many more-energy-efficient technologies that promise to raise the economic output per kilogram of carbon emitted.

Another way of increasing world carbon efficiency is to replace fossil fuels with renewable sources of energy. Here the most immediately promising new technology is wind power, as mentioned earlier. In 1992, wind generators produced enough electricity in the United States—mostly in California—to have satisfied the residential needs of San Francisco and Washington, D.C. With recent advances in the efficiency with which turbines convert wind into electricity, the stage is set for rapid growth in the use of wind power throughout the world.

BICYCLES LEAVE CARS
BEHIND

One of the most visible shifts in the world economy following the oil price hikes was the slower growth in automobile production and the accelerated growth in bicycle output. Many people living in western industrial countries are surprised to learn that bicycles used for transportation now greatly outnumber automobiles. But in China, with a population far greater than that of the industrial West, bicycles outnumber automobiles by 250 to 1. Indeed, in Asia, where more than half the world's people live, bicycle ownership dwarfs that of cars. In contrast to the United States, where bicycles are often used for recreational purposes, in Asia they are a basic means of transportation—a low-cost source of greater mobility.

In 1950, automobile production totalled 8 million, while that of bicycles was 11 million.

(See pp. 86–89.) During the sixties, however, as rebuilding economies shifted into high gear, auto production climbed rapidly—and by the end of the decade it had reached 23 million, compared with 25 million for bicycles. At that point, many thought cars would soon eclipse bicycles.

Three events in quick succession changed the outlook dramatically. First was the growing environmental awareness that unfolded during the late sixties and early seventies. This contributed to an abrupt doubling of bicycle production between 1969 and 1973, from 25 million to 52 million. Then the 1973 oil price shock hit the automobile industry hard. And by the time it had recovered in 1979, it was hit with the second oil price hike, which again dropped production.

In 1992, 35 million cars rolled off the assembly lines—not much more than the 30 million produced in 1973. Bicycle production, meanwhile, had climbed to 100 million, increasing the production ratio between these two modes of transport to nearly three to one and further establishing the bicycle's position as the world's leading vehicle for personal transportation. (See Figure 3.)

The principal reason so many more bicycles than cars are produced is that an automobile costs 100 times as much. In addition to the purchase price, the cost of auto ownership includes fuel, maintenance, insurance, and parking. The bottom line is that over the last two decades the number of people who have reached the "automobile level of affluence" has remained relatively small; less than 10 percent of the world's people can afford cars, whereas an estimated 80 percent can buy bikes. That ratio of affordability is unlikely to change in the near future.

As mayors and city planners become disenchanted with the automobile, constraints on its use will increase the reliance on public transport and bicycles. In Amsterdam, city plan-

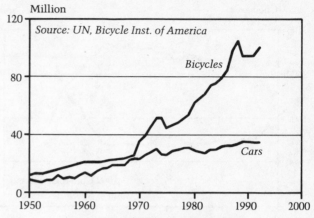

Figure 3: World Automobile and Bicycle Production, 1950–92

ners are now phasing out cars, limiting the use of motorized vehicles only to public transportation and freight deliveries. As more and more city governments restrict automobile use, particularly in large cities, such as Rome and Mexico City, the attraction of owning a car will diminish further.

World auto production appears unlikely to grow much in the foreseeable future while the production of bicycles will probably continue at a high level. Increasing personal mobility may now depend much more on bicycles than cars.

USING TAX POLICY TO
REVERSE TRENDS

One of the most promising recent trends is the willingness of national governments to use tax policy not only to raise revenue but also to reverse destructive trends, such as cigarette smoking or the burning of fossil fuels. Nowhere is this more evident or successful than in the use of tax policy to discourage smoking, a habit that the World Health Organization (WHO) estimates will claim 21 million lives over the next decade in the industrial world alone.

WHO points to a reduction in cigarette smoking as the easiest way to eliminate large

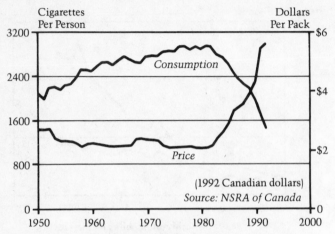

Figure 4: Cigarette Consumption Per Person and Real Price of a Pack of 20 Cigarettes, Canada, 1950–92

numbers of unnecessary deaths. In 1992, the number of cigarettes produced per person dropped 1.7 percent, and in 1991, 2.7 percent. (See pp. 98–99.) All told, the number dropped 4.4 percent from 1990 to 1992, the largest such drop since records of smoking began at mid-century.

Several factors account for this drop. The global recession is making it difficult for some people to maintain their habit. Declines in purchasing power in the former Soviet Union and Eastern Europe are also reducing consumption. Governments, medical associations, and public interest groups are promoting antismoking campaigns for health reasons.

At the policy level, many governments are taxing cigarettes for health reasons. (See pp. 116–17.) In three countries, the tax per pack is now above $3. Denmark has the highest tax at $3.68, followed by Norway at $3.33 and Canada at $3.01. In these countries, a pack of 20 cigarettes now costs between $4.33 and $4.87.

In Canada, where taxes were raised from 38¢ per pack in 1980 to $3.01 in 1992, the average price for 20 cigarettes is now $4.34. This has reduced smoking dramatically, cutting the number of cigarettes per person by nearly half between 1980 and 1992. (See Figure 4.)

A continuing flow of U.S. research studies has documented the social cost of cigarette smoking. In the United States, secondhand cigarette smoke claims nearly 1,000 lives per week, more than are lost to automobile accidents. All told, the U.S. Centers for Disease Control and Prevention places the annual loss from smoking at 434,000 lives.

Public attention focuses on lung cancer, but this accounts for only one fourth of smoking-related deaths. Smoking also increases the incidence of esophagal, pancreatic, cervical, bladder, kidney and other cancers. By far the heaviest toll comes from cardiovascular disease—including heart attacks and strokes—which claims 201,000 lives each year.

The U.S. Office of Technology Assessment estimates the cost of health care and of lost productivity from smoking-related illnesses at $65 billion a year. This helps explain why lifetime health care costs are some $6,000 higher for smokers than for nonsmokers. As information on the costs of smoking, including health care and lower worker productivity, spreads, more and more governments will tax cigarettes at a level that reflects their cost to society. The worldwide rate of cigarette smoking is likely to continue the decline of the past few years.

Whether the goal is to reduce cigarette smoking, stabilize climate, or reduce air pollution, tax policy is emerging as the most promising instrument of public policy. In an age when our future so clearly depends on protecting our natural life-support systems, lowering taxes on constructive activities, such as income from work or from savings, and raising them on environmentally destructive activities, such as the burning of fossil fuels, the use of virgin raw materials, or the generation of hazardous waste, is both eminently sensible and increasingly appealing. If governments do turn to tax policy to curb environmentally destructive activities, a number of damaging trends could be reversed, generating even more discontinuities than are now in prospect.

Part **ONE**

Key Indicators

Food Trends

The 1992 world grain harvest totalled 1,745 million tons, up 3 percent from the preceding year.[1] (See Figure 1.) This boosted output per person 1 percent, but still left it 8 percent below the historical high reached in 1984.[2] (See Figure 2.)

These global figures mask vivid contrasts in the 1992 harvest among countries and regions, with the clearest one being that between the bumper U.S. grain harvest and the drought-reduced harvests in sub-Saharan Africa.

The United States had an unusually heavy grain harvest largely because exceptionally favorable weather boosted corn yields to an all-time high of 121 bushels per acre.[3] In recent years, the country has normally harvested about 300 million tons of grain, roughly 200 million of corn and 100 million of the other grains—wheat, sorghum, barley, rye, and rice. In 1992, the corn harvest soared to 237 million tons.[4]

Africa, meanwhile, experienced one of the most devastating droughts in its history. Harvests suffered throughout the southern part of the continent, in East Africa, and in parts of West Africa. Normally, South Africa and Zimbabwe harvest far more grain than they can consume domestically and export a large share of their crop to other countries in the region and beyond. In 1992, however, the harvest was cut so dramatically that both countries had to import to meet their own needs.[5] In turn, countries traditionally dependent on them for grain faced famine-threatening shortages. They were forced to import grain from outside the region, a logistically difficult undertaking in an area where the transportation system is not well developed.[6]

In East Africa, drought affected Somalia, the Sudan, Ethiopia, and Kenya, but was concentrated in Somalia, where national government disintegration and warring tribal factions interfered with food relief efforts. As a result, hundreds of Somalis were dying daily in the summer and fall of 1992—a situation that led to emergency relief actions. In the Sudan, also plagued by drought and civil war, the Food and Agriculture Organization reported deaths from malnutrition-related diseases in the southern part of the country.[7]

Drought is not new in Africa, but the capacity of the natural systems to deal with it has diminished. Land is degraded from deforestation, overgrazing, overplowing, and erosion. Topsoils thinned by erosion and low in organic matter store little moisture to carry through a period of extended drought. As a result, the effects of drought are far more devastating today than they were a generation ago.[8]

Northern Europe also suffered from drought in 1992. Among the countries affected were Norway, Denmark, Sweden, Germany, Poland, Finland, Estonia, Latvia, and Lithuania. Although grain harvests were cut in half in some of these countries, shortfalls were easily offset with imported grain.[9]

Harvest trends diverged within the former Soviet bloc. While harvests were down throughout Eastern Europe, ranging from a drop of 12 percent in Czechoslovakia to 31 percent in Poland, output was up sharply in the Commonwealth of Independent States (CIS).[10] The 1992 CIS grain harvest totalled 182 million tons, up from 152 million tons the year before, a rise of nearly 20 percent.[11] Kazakhstan, favored with unusually abundant rainfall, harvested a record 32 million tons of grain, 3 percent above its previous record of 31 million tons in 1979.[12]

Within the CIS, the nature of the food problem has changed. It is no longer so much a matter of supply as it is purchasing power. With subsidies removed, grain prices have risen at a time when the unemployed, part-time workers, pensioners, and single heads of household are struggling to make ends meet.[13]

In addition to the droughts and economic reforms that are wreaking short-term havoc in many countries, several longer term trends are slowing the growth in world food output: growth in the world grain area came to a halt in 1981, the irrigated area per person has been declining since 1979, and world fertilizer use has actually dropped in recent years, reversing the long-term trend of rapid growth.[14]

WORLD GRAIN PRODUCTION, 1950–92

YEAR	TOTAL (mill. tons)	PER CAPITA (kilograms)
1950	631	247
1951	645	249
1952	704	267
1953	717	268
1954	709	260
1955	759	273
1956	794	280
1957	784	271
1958	849	288
1959	834	278
1960	847	279
1961	822	267
1962	864	276
1963	865	270
1964	921	281
1965	917	274
1966	1,005	294
1967	1,029	295
1968	1,069	301
1969	1,078	297
1970	1,096	296
1971	1,194	316
1972	1,156	299
1973	1,272	323
1974	1,220	304
1975	1,250	306
1976	1,363	328
1977	1,337	316
1978	1,467	341
1979	1,428	326
1980	1,447	325
1981	1,499	331
1982	1,550	336
1983	1,486	317
1984	1,649	346
1985	1,664	343
1986	1,683	341
1987	1,612	321
1988	1,564	306
1989	1,685	324
1990	1,780	336
1991	1,696	315
1992 (prel)	1,745	318

SOURCE: USDA, *World Grain Database*, (unpublished printouts) (Washington, D.C.: 1991); USDA, *World Grain Situation and Outlook*, Washington, D.C., March 1993.

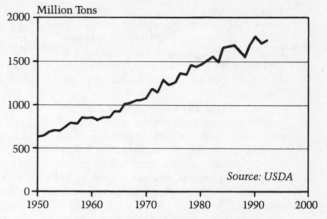

Figure 1: World Grain Production, 1950–92

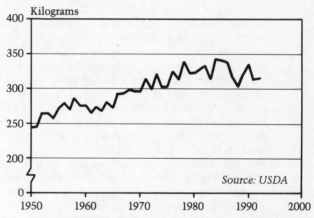

Figure 2: World Grain Production Per Person, 1950–92

Soybean Harvest Sets Record Lester R. Brown

Weighing in at nearly 114 million tons, the 1992 world soybean harvest set a new record—up 7 percent from the previous record of 107 million tons set in 1989.[1] (See Figure 1.) Despite these impressive overall gains in production of the world's leading protein crop, output per person is no longer increasing.[2] (See Figure 2.)

From 1950 to 1979, the soybean harvest multiplied more than fivefold, expanding at nearly 6 percent per year. During the following 13 years, however, output expanded by only 17 percent, or little more than 1 percent per year. Per person, soybean output tripled between 1950 and 1979, climbing from 7 kilograms to 21 kilograms. Since then, though, it has fluctuated between 18 and 21 kilograms and in 1992 was still 3 percent below the all-time high of 21.4 kilograms set in 1979.[3]

Soybeans are the world's leading source of both vegetable oil and protein meal. Once grown for their oil content, they are now cultivated primarily as a source of protein, specifically for the meal left after they are crushed and oil has been extracted. Although the oil is widely used for cooking, the more valuable meal is used throughout the world as a protein supplement in livestock and poultry rations.

Four countries—the United States, Brazil, Argentina, and China—accounted for nearly 90 percent of the 1992 crop. Of these, the United States was the dominant producer and exporter, bringing in just over half the world harvest.[4]

The 1992 U.S. harvest of 57 million tons was the third largest on record, although it was well below the 68 million tons of 1979.[5] At $11 billion, the soybean crop is a cornerstone of the U.S. farm economy, worth nearly twice as much as the wheat harvest. Only corn outranks soybeans in value—just narrowly—among crops grown in the United States.[6]

The key to the bumper 1992 U.S. harvest was an unprecedented yield of 2.53 tons per hectare, a record due almost entirely to exceptionally favorable weather.[7] With one of the coolest summers in years, both temperature and soil moisture growing conditions were ideal throughout the growing season.

Long consumed directly in China as a food,

usually in the form of bean curd, the soybean rose from obscurity to its position as the world's leading oilseed because of the growth in demand for meat, milk, cheese, and eggs. As the demand for these livestock products soared after mid-century, so too did the need for soybean meal.

Two of the dominant production trends in the world soybean economy contrast sharply. The Latin American harvest has expanded rapidly while the Chinese harvest has stagnated, increasing little over the last 40 years.[8] In trade, the notable trend has been the soaring import demand in the rapidly growing East Asian economies of Taiwan, South Korea, the Philippines, Indonesia, Malaysia, and Thailand.[9]

The source of rising soybean output contrasts sharply with that of grains. Since mid-century, some four fifths of the growth in the world grain harvest has come from raising yield per hectare.[10] For soybeans, however, it has come largely from expanding the area planted: Since 1950, the soybean yield has risen roughly two thirds, from 1.2 tons per hectare to nearly 2 tons. But the area in soybeans has nearly quadrupled, going from 15 million hectares to 56 million.[11]

Soybeans are the only major crop for which farmers depend primarily on expanding the planted area to expand output. Cereals are highly responsive to the application of chemical fertilizer, particularly nitrogenous fertilizer, but the soybean—a legume—fixes much of its own nitrogen and is much less responsive to chemical fertilizer.

With the grasslands that support cattle, sheep, and goats now fully used or, in many countries, overused, continued growth in output of meat, milk, cheese, and other livestock products is closely tied to feeding grain.[12] To do this efficiently requires a protein supplement, typically soybean meal. Future gains in livestock output are thus keyed to the ability of the world's farmers to keep expanding soybean output, a difficult undertaking in a land-scarce world.

WORLD SOYBEAN PRODUCTION, 1950–92

YEAR	TOTAL (mill. tons)	PER CAPITA (kilograms)
1950	18	7
1951	17	7
1952	18	7
1953	18	7
1954	20	7
1955	21	8
1956	24	8
1957	25	9
1958	28	10
1959	28	9
1960	27	9
1961	31	10
1962	31	10
1963	32	10
1964	32	10
1965	37	11
1966	39	11
1967	41	12
1968	44	12
1969	45	12
1970	46	12
1971	48	13
1972	49	13
1973	62	16
1974	55	14
1975	66	16
1976	59	14
1977	72	17
1978	78	18
1979	94	21
1980	81	18
1981	86	19
1982	94	20
1983	83	18
1984	93	19
1985	97	20
1986	98	20
1987	104	21
1988	96	19
1989	107	21
1990	104	20
1991	106	20
1992 (prel)	114	21

SOURCES: USDA, *World Oilseed Database* (unpublished printouts) (Washington, D.C.: 1991); *World Oilseed Situation and Outlook Report*, February 1993.

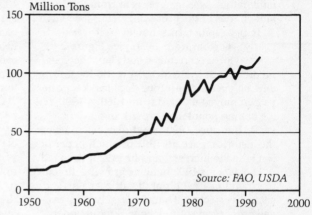

Figure 1: World Soybean Production, 1950–92

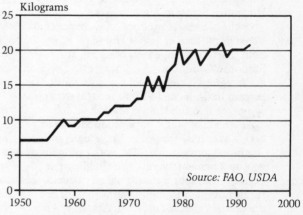

Figure 2: World Soybean Production Per Person, 1950–92

Meat Production Up Slightly   Lester R. Brown

World meat production in 1992, totalling 176 million tons, was up 1 percent from the 174 million tons of the preceding year.[1] (See Figure 1.) In per capita terms, however, it was down nearly 1 percent from 1991. (See Figure 2.)

Few global economic trends have been as predictable as the growth in world meat production over the past four decades. Year after year, it moved upward from 1950 to 1990, falling behind population growth in only six years. But since 1990 growth has fallen below the historical pace; in 1991 production per person failed to increase, and in 1992 it declined.[2]

The data for 1992 indicate growing difficulty in expanding the output of cattle, sheep, and goats, livestock that subsist largely on grass and other forms of roughage. Production of beef fell in 1992 by 2 percent, while mutton was unchanged, leading to per capita declines of 4 and 2 percent, respectively. (See Figure 3.) World beef production per person fell to 9.4 kilograms, the lowest in 30 years.[3]

Declines in meat production were concentrated in the former Soviet Union (− 12 percent), Eastern Europe (− 6 percent), and the European Community (− 1 percent).[4] Drops in these regions largely offset a robust gain of 7 percent in China and a more modest expansion of 4 percent in the United States.[5]

An excess of world pork production over beef that first developed in the late seventies continued to widen in 1992. Pork production was up 2 percent overall, thus holding per capita consumption steady, largely because of surging output in China.[6] Gains in pork production of 7 percent in North America, 3 percent in Latin America, and 6 percent in China more than offset the declines of 15 percent in the former Soviet Union and 3 percent in Eastern Europe, the third consecutive drop in both cases.[7]

Poultry output, meanwhile, continued its rapid climb, rising more than 4 percent in total or 2 percent per person.[8] As with other meats, poultry output fell in the former Soviet Union and Eastern Europe, by 9 and 4 percent, respectively. Three consecutive years of decline have dropped poultry production in the former Soviet Union by 16 percent from the 1989 high.[9]

Unified Germany boosted poultry output in 1992, after two years of decline, as integration of the industry in the two Germanies neared completion.[10] Declining meat production in Eastern Europe and the former Soviet Union can be traced to the removal of subsidies that kept grain and meat prices artificially low and to falls in overall purchasing power.[11]

Cattle, sheep, and goats—all ruminants—have the invaluable capacity to convert grass, hay, leaves, and other such materials into edible products, such as meat, milk, and cheese. With nearly all the world's rangeland now fully used and with the productivity of some of it falling because of overgrazing, maintaining the historical growth in the output of grassland-based meat is no longer possible.[12] Worldwide, the effect of this natural constraint on both beef and mutton production is becoming more clear with each additional year's data.

Pigs and chickens, lacking the capacity to subsist on roughage, depend on concentrated feeds, such as grain and soybean meal. Once grazing capacity is exhausted, additional meat output comes almost entirely from grain and soybeans, the production of which is still expanding.

When the potential for expanded grazing is exhausted, the advantage shifts from ruminants to animals with a single stomach, which are more efficient at converting grain into meat. Beef cattle in the feedlot typically require seven pounds of grain to add a pound of weight. Pigs require roughly four pounds, whereas chickens can add a pound with scarcely two pounds of grain.[13] The rapid growth in poultry production and the prospect that it could overtake beef before the end of this decade reflects the strong competitive advantage of poultry and a growing preference for poultry over red meat for health reasons.

The decline in per capita meat production since 1990 may be a temporary interruption of a trend that is about to resume its upward climb. Or it could be a signal that the limits of grazing capacity, combined with falling per capita grain production and static per capita soybean production, are bringing the era of rising meat consumption per person to an end.

WORLD MEAT PRODUCTION, 1950–92

YEAR	TOTAL (mill. tons)	PER CAPITA (kilograms)
1950	46	18.0
1951	50	19.3
1952	53	20.1
1953	56	20.9
1954	58	21.3
1955	60	21.6
1956	63	22.2
1957	65	22.5
1958	67	22.8
1959	69	23.0
1960	68	22.4
1961	70	22.7
1962	73	23.3
1963	77	24.0
1964	78	23.8
1965	82	24.5
1966	86	25.2
1967	90	25.8
1968	93	26.2
1969	94	25.9
1970	98	26.5
1971	102	27.0
1972	105	27.2
1973	106	26.9
1974	112	27.9
1975	113	27.7
1976	116	27.9
1977	120	28.4
1978	125	29.0
1979	129	29.5
1980	133	29.9
1981	136	30.0
1982	137	29.7
1983	142	30.3
1984	145	30.4
1985	150	30.9
1986	156	31.6
1987	161	32.0
1988	164	32.1
1989	167	32.1
1990	171	32.3
1991	174	32.3
1992 (prel)	176	32.1

SOURCES: FAO, *1948–1985 World Crop and Livestock Statistics* (Rome: 1987); FAO, *FAO Production Yearbooks 1988–1991*; USDA, *World Agricultural Production,* August 1992 and March 1993; Worldwatch estimates.

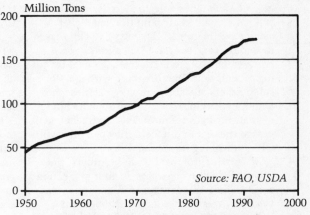

Figure 1: World Meat Production, 1950–92

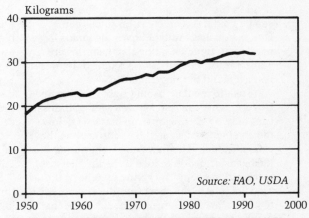

Figure 2: World Meat Production Per Person, 1950–92

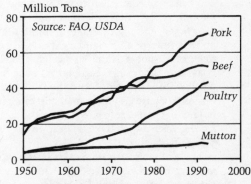

Figure 3: World Meat Production by Type, 1950–92

Fish Catch No Longer Growing Hal Kane

The world fish catch dropped from its 1989 high of 100 million tons to 97 million in 1990 and has remained at about that level ever since.[1] (See Figure 1.) Harvests have increased in some oceans but have fallen in others. And rising catches of some species are offset by falling catches of others. Breaking with a historical trend of constantly growing catches, stagnation in the global catch now appears likely to continue because most seas have reached or passed the maximum yield they can offer without diminishing future harvests.[2]

Because of growing human numbers, the fish available per person is declining. (See Figure 2.) The 17.8 kilograms a person now harvested by the world's fishers is 8 percent below its 1988 record, and is below the level it had reached in 1968. Growth per capita was rapid in the fifties and sixties, but the per capita yield has scarcely risen since then.[3] Overfishing has brought down the yields in many seas, demonstrating that fisheries are a natural resource that can be reduced (by mismanagement) but not expanded.

A rush to regulate fishing rights has begun. Governments can protect their fishing industries only by keeping marine harvests below the level where fish are taken faster than they can reproduce. The European Community (EC) has decided to reduce its fishing fleet by at least 20 percent.[4] By giving up tens of thousands of jobs in the short run, Europeans hope to protect an even larger number of jobs that would disappear if fish stocks collapsed.

Canada and the EC have both suspended cod fishing off Canadian coasts.[5] Iceland will restrict its cod catch to 40 percent less than it now takes, although cod has accounted for about a third of all Icelandic exports.[6] In order to enforce quotas, Namibia has banned foreign boats from its waters, and Sierra Leone has partially followed suit.[7] And the South Pacific Forum Fisheries Agency, made up of eight island nations, has restricted Asian and U.S. fishing vessels to 200 boats, despite angry complaints from abroad.[8]

The need to constrain fishers stems from what an EC official has called "chronic over-capacity"—the ability of fishing fleets to take far more than nature has to offer.[9] Massive "factory" boats use high-tech electronics to track fish, and more vessels harvest the seas. Competition among fishers spurs them to grab as much as they can as quickly as they can with little regard for the long-term maintenance of their bounty.[10] Severe overfishing can change the composition of marine life, as some species gain advantages over others, possibly leading to extinction.

Overfishing is not the only bane of sea life today. Some 90 percent (by mass) of marine animals rely on coastal areas such as wetlands, mangrove swamps, or rivers for spawning grounds. But well over half the original area of mangroves in tropical countries has been lost, and in industrial countries, the rate for wetlands loss is just as high. In Italy, it is 95 percent.[11]

About a third of the world's urban population lives within 60 kilometers of a coastline, a big contributor to the pollution that reaches the seas. Heavy metals have polluted fish and damaged the health of people who ate them. Sewage, fertilizers, and runoff from agriculture have overfed algae, causing it to "bloom" in a rapid growth that uses up the oxygen that fish need to breathe. Estimates of global annual discharge into rivers range from 7 million to 35 million tons of nitrogen and from 600,000 to 3.75 million tons of dissolved phosphorus.[12]

Stratospheric ozone depletion that lets through more ultraviolet radiation also affects life in the sea. The photosynthesis and growth of phytoplankton, which form the lowest link of the food chain, have decreased by as much as 20 percent near the surface of Antarctic waters—and the surface is where most marine growth and reproduction takes place.[13] Global warming also may touch sea life deeply because it could alter ocean currents, which circulate heat and vital nutrients.

After adding an average of 2 million tons to the world's food supply each year from 1950 to 1989, fisheries may have ceased to be a major source of more food.[14]

WORLD FISH CATCH, 1950–92

YEAR	TOTAL (mill. tons)	PER CAPITA (kilograms)
1950	22	8.6
1951	26	10.0
1952	25	9.5
1953	26	9.7
1954	27	9.9
1955	29	10.4
1956	30	10.6
1957	31	10.7
1958	33	11.2
1959	36	12.0
1960	38	12.5
1961	42	13.6
1962	45	14.4
1963	48	15.0
1964	53	16.2
1965	54	16.1
1966	57	16.7
1967	60	17.2
1968	64	18.0
1969	63	17.4
1970	66	17.8
1971	66	17.5
1972	62	16.1
1973	63	16.0
1974	67	16.7
1975	66	16.2
1976	69	16.6
1977	70	16.5
1978	70	16.3
1979	71	16.2
1980	72	16.2
1981	75	16.6
1982	77	16.7
1983	78	16.6
1984	84	17.6
1985	86	17.7
1986	92	18.6
1987	93	18.5
1988	99	19.4
1989	100	19.2
1990	97	18.3
1991	97	18.0
1992 (prel)	97	17.8

SOURCE: FAO, *Yearbook of Fishery Statistics: Catches and Landings* (Rome: various years); 1991 and 1992 data from FAO, Rome, private communications, April 29, 1993.

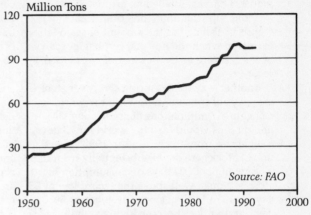

Figure 1: World Fish Catch, 1950–92

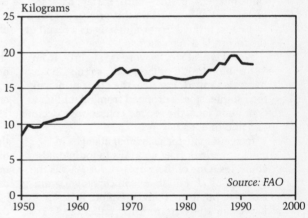

Figure 2: World Fish Catch Per Person, 1950–92

Grain Stocks Increase
Lester R. Brown

World carryover stocks of grain at the start of the 1993 harvest totalled an estimated 341 million tons, up 19 million tons from 1992.[1] (See Figure 1.) Defined as the amount of grain left in the bin when the new harvest begins, carryover stocks are a key measure of world food security.

Another way of measuring carryover stocks is in days of consumption. With the world using up 4.7 million tons of grain a day, 341 million tons would feed the world for 73 days, a slight rise from the 69 days in 1992.[2] (See Figure 2.) Stocks are down substantially from the all-time high of 104 days of consumption in 1987, although well above the record low of 55 days in 1973.[3] When stocks drop below 60 days, grain prices become highly volatile, sometimes even doubling, as they did between 1972 and 1973.[4]

Nearly all the rise in world grain stocks came in coarse grains—corn, barley, oats, sorghum, and millet. Within this group, the gain was concentrated in corn, mostly as a result of the record U.S. harvest.[5]

World wheat stocks were up slightly, from 131 million to 136 million tons, as the 1992 harvest climbed. For rice, the other principal food staple, stocks dropped from 67 million to 64 million tons, the second consecutive decline of 3 million tons.[6]

In geographic terms, global changes in stocks overlook rises and falls in individual countries. One of the surprises for 1993 is the increase of 11 million tons in carryover grain stocks in the former Soviet Union. A better harvest in 1992, up from 152 million to 182 million tons, plus a reduction in livestock herds combined to boost stocks.[7]

As prices of grain fed to livestock in the former Soviet republics moved up toward world market levels following market reforms, the prices of meat, milk, and eggs went up, cutting consumption. In addition, uncertainty about feedgrain supplies led farmers to reduce livestock numbers sharply. The resulting decline in grain use both lifted grain stocks and lowered grain imports.[8]

While grain stocks were building in the former Soviet Union, they were being decimated in southern Africa by what may have been the worst drought of the century. The harvest of corn, the principal staple, was reduced by 73 percent in South Africa and 68 percent in Zimbabwe, the two countries that traditionally produce surpluses for shipment to the other countries in the region and that maintain much of the region's stocks.[9]

Though a useful indicator of food security, global carryover stocks do not tell the entire picture. A more complete sense of the situation requires a look at changes in income. The fall in income during the eighties in some 49 countries containing 846 million people almost certainly reduced food consumption in those areas.[10] Since there was no substantial drop in food prices nor a major increase in food aid to these nations, food consumption per person must have declined among hundreds of millions of people. Unfortunately, the drops in income are concentrated in the poorest countries, where there are few, if any, national food consumption surveys to measure precise changes in food intake.

In southern Africa, the severe drought that sharply reduced the maize harvest was partly offset by dramatic increases in imports and in food relief efforts. Nonetheless, hunger increased in many countries in the region during 1992.[11]

In some countries, such as Somalia, where the harvest was decimated by a combination of drought and civil war, grain stocks were negligible. The results were calamitous. Few countries have ever faced the degree of food insecurity and starvation that gripped Somalia during the last half of 1992. Only the arrival of several hundred U.N. troops in the fall of 1992, followed by some 40,000 U.S. troops, could stabilize the country politically. This in turn permitted the distribution of large enough quantities of food to arrest the heavy loss of life.

WORLD GRAIN CARRYOVER STOCKS, 1963–93[1]

YEAR	STOCKS (mill. tons)	(days use)
1963	190	81
1964	193	82
1965	194	77
1966	159	61
1967	190	71
1968	213	77
1969	244	86
1970	228	76
1971	193	62
1972	217	68
1973	180	55
1974	192	56
1975	200	60
1976	220	65
1977	280	78
1978	278	77
1979	328	84
1980	315	81
1981	288	71
1982	309	77
1983	357	87
1984	304	72
1985	366	85
1986	434	100
1987	465	104
1988	409	90
1989	316	70
1990	301	65
1991	342	73
1992	322	69
1993 (prel)	341	73

[1]Data are for year when new harvest begins.
SOURCE: USDA, *World Grain Situation and Outlook*, December 1992.

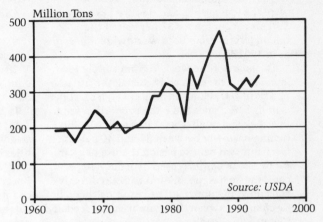

Figure 1: World Grain Carryover Stocks, 1963–93

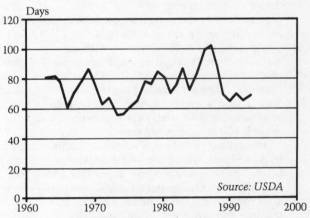

Figure 2: World Grain Carryover Stocks as Days of Consumption, 1963–93

Grain Used for Feed Unchanged
Lester R. Brown

In 1992, an estimated 635 million tons of grain were fed to livestock and poultry.[1] (See Figure 1.) This accounted for 37 percent of the 1.72 billion tons of grain used worldwide, the same as in 1991.[2]

The share of the world's grain supply fed to animals increased steadily during the fifties and sixties, reaching an all-time high of 41 percent in 1972. Since then, the proportion fed to livestock and poultry has changed little, fluctuating narrowly between 37 and 40 percent. Over this two-decade period the use of grain for livestock has increased by nearly 40 percent. But so has the amount of grain directly consumed by humans. The result has been little change between the share used for feed and that used for food.[3]

Corn (maize), much of it grown in the United States, accounts for the lion's share of world feedgrain use.[4] Barley and wheat used directly for feed, along with milling by-products of wheat and rice, account for most of the remaining grain used for feed.[5]

Not surprisingly, the countries with the highest per capita grain use are those where people consume large quantities of livestock products. Among the leaders are the United States, Canada, and the former Soviet Union. In all three, grain use per person approaches or exceeds 800 kilograms per year.[6]

At the other end of the spectrum are countries like India, where grain consumption is below 200 kilograms per person per year.[7] At this level, roughly one pound a day, nearly all grain must be consumed directly merely to maintain minimal levels of physical activity. With such limited availability, only 2 percent of the grain in India is fed to livestock.[8]

The world's three leading users of feedgrain account for just over half of world use: the United States (151 million tons), the former Soviet Union (136 million tons), and China (64 million tons). Brazil, Canada, Poland, Japan, and France each use between 15 million and 23 million tons.[9]

Feedgrain use per person is highest in countries that export meat. In Denmark, a heavy exporter of pork, some 82 percent of all grain used is for feed.[10] In the 12 countries in the European Community, 57 percent of grain is fed to livestock and poultry.[11]

Only when countries reach middle-income levels can they afford to feed more grain to livestock and poultry than to people. Brazil, for example, first crossed this threshold in 1979, when 51 percent of its grain was fed to animals. By 1990, the figure had edged up to 55 percent.[12]

In the rapidly growing economies of East Asia, the amount fed to animals is climbing steadily. In Taiwan, which exports large quantities of pork, the figure has reached 62 percent, a level higher than in some countries in Europe. In South Korea, another rapid-growth country, the share of grain fed to animals climbed from just over 2 percent in 1960 to 39 percent in 1990.[13]

In Mexico, the share has gone from 5 percent in 1960 to 31 percent in 1990. During the same period, Japan climbed from 14 to 47 percent, a figure that would be even higher if Japan were not importing substantial amounts of beef and pork.[14]

Growth in China's feed use has accelerated sharply since the economic reforms of 1978. In that year, only 8 percent of grain was used for animal feed, but by 1990 the figure had climbed to 20 percent, much of it used to produce pork.[15]

Worldwide, the amount of grain per person available to produce meat, milk, and eggs does not seem likely to rise much, if at all, during the nineties. (See Figure 2.) The shortage of new cropland, the growing scarcity of fresh water, and the lack of any dramatic new yield-raising technologies have slowed the growth in world grain output markedly over the last several years. On the demand side, mounting concern in western industrial societies over the possible adverse health effects of eating too much meat is also constraining growth in consumption.

With the global increase in population almost certainly exceeding that in per capita income during the nineties, the amount of grain needed for food is likely to expand faster than that needed for feed. If so, the share of the world grain harvest fed to animals could drop below the 37–40 percent of the last two decades.

WORLD GRAIN USE AND SHARE
FED TO LIVESTOCK, 1960–92

YEAR	TOTAL GRAIN USE (mill. tons)	GRAIN USED FOR FEED (mill. tons)	SHARE (percent)
1960	822	289	35
1961	823	288	35
1962	845	288	34
1963	851	289	34
1964	908	310	34
1965	940	344	37
1966	958	355	37
1967	991	371	37
1968	1,022	391	38
1969	1,080	417	39
1970	1,113	426	38
1971	1,153	461	40
1972	1,178	478	41
1973	1,241	488	39
1974	1,196	446	37
1975	1,216	454	37
1976	1,283	481	37
1977	1,321	504	38
1978	1,396	547	39
1979	1,423	565	40
1980	1,456	552	38
1981	1,461	566	39
1982	1,483	584	39
1983	1,512	576	38
1984	1,570	604	38
1985	1,577	615	39
1986	1,632	648	40
1987	1,650	650	39
1988	1,639	627	38
1989	1,683	631	37
1990	1,718	660	38
1991	1,713	633	37
1992 (prel)	1,725	635	37

SOURCES: USDA, *World Grain Database*
(unpublished printout) (Washington, D.C.: 1992);
FAO, *Food Outlook,* March 1993.

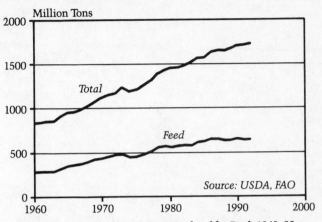

Figure 1: World Grain Use, Total and for Feed, 1960–92

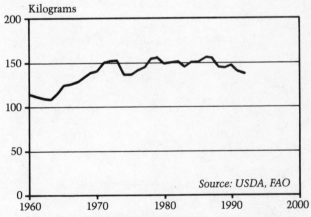

Figure 2: World Per Capita Grain Fed to Livestock, 1960–92

Agricultural Resource
Trends

Grain Area Unchanged   Lester R. Brown

In 1992, the world's farmers harvested 695 million hectares of grain, an area essentially unchanged from the three preceding years.[1] (See Figure 1.) The area harvested in 1992 was some 5 percent less than the all-time high of 735 million hectares in 1981.[2]

In per capita terms, the grain harvested area has been shrinking steadily since mid-century. (See Figure 2.) At that time, the world had 0.23 hectares per person to meet the needs for grain. In 1992, the number was less than 0.13 hectares, scarcely half the mid-century total.[3]

In many ways, the 1981 figure of land harvested was unrealistically high because it included a substantial area, particularly in the United States and the Soviet Union, that was highly erodible and should not have been plowed. The high grain prices of the middle and late seventies had encouraged farmers to plow land that should have been left in grass. During the decade since, this fast eroding land has either gone back to grass or simply been abandoned as its productivity drained away.[4]

Worldwide, gains in cropland area from year to year are the result of various cropland expansion initiatives, including the conversion of forest to cropland, new irrigation projects that permit the farming of land otherwise too dry to farm, and drainage of wetlands. Forest conversion is concentrated in such places as the outer islands of Indonesia (part of a long-term resettlement program of people from densely populated Java) and the Amazon regions of Brazil and other Latin American countries. Some of these gains are illusory, since this land will often sustain cultivation for only a few years before losing its natural fertility.

Some of the most important gains in grain harvested area during the last 25 years have come from the adoption of high-yielding, early maturing wheats and rices.[5] Traditional geography texts contained agricultural maps with a line drawn across both India and China, separating the wheat- and rice-growing regions. Modern maps do not make that distinction: wheat has extended into rice-growing areas and vice versa, with rice being grown in the summer and wheat in the winter. Earlier maturing varieties of both grains, combined with the spread of irrigation that facilitated

cropping during the dry season, helped increase double cropping. This, in turn, expanded the grain harvested area, even though the net area in grain did not expand.

On the opposite side of the ledger, the requirements of an additional 91 million people each year for housing, schools, and transportation reduces the area available for crops.[6] Land claimed by expanding transportation systems is particularly extensive. For example, the growth in the world automobile fleet means cropland is paved over for streets, highways, and parking lots. Some 200 square feet is needed merely to park an automobile. If a car is to be widely used, parking spaces must be available in many different places: near residences, workplaces, shops, and recreation areas. Assuming a minimum of two parking spaces per car, the land required to park 100 cars could easily produce one ton of grain per year.[7]

In China, which in some years produces even more grain than the United States does, the principal threat to cropland comes from conversion to nonfarm uses. The nonfarm land needs of a population of 1.1 billion people for new houses, factories, schools, and roads are reducing China's cropland area by an estimated 1 percent every two years, a loss the country can ill afford.[8]

From 1950 to 1981 the world grain harvested area expanded some 24 percent, or nearly 0.7 percent per year.[9] This accounted for roughly one fourth of the growth in grain output, while raising land productivity provided the remaining three fourths. Since 1981, the increase in output has come only from raising land productivity, helping to explain why the growth in the grain harvest has slowed so dramatically.

If world population grows as projected, the grain area per person in the year 2000 will likely be less than half what it was in 1950. Perhaps more disturbing, the cropland area per person is expected to continue shrinking throughout the early decades of the twenty-first century.

WORLD GRAIN HARVESTED AREA, 1950–92

YEAR	TOTAL (mill. hectares)	PER CAPITA (hectares)
1950	593	0.23
1951	595	0.23
1952	615	0.23
1953	626	0.23
1954	634	0.23
1955	646	0.23
1956	655	0.23
1957	651	0.23
1958	653	0.22
1959	642	0.21
1960	651	0.21
1961	647	0.21
1962	655	0.21
1963	660	0.21
1964	660	0.20
1965	657	0.20
1966	659	0.19
1967	669	0.19
1968	674	0.19
1969	675	0.19
1970	666	0.18
1971	675	0.18
1972	664	0.17
1973	691	0.18
1974	693	0.17
1975	711	0.17
1976	719	0.17
1977	716	0.17
1978	716	0.17
1979	713	0.16
1980	724	0.16
1981	735	0.16
1982	718	0.16
1983	709	0.15
1984	712	0.15
1985	717	0.15
1986	711	0.14
1987	686	0.14
1988	690	0.13
1989	696	0.13
1990	695	0.13
1991	693	0.13
1992 (prel)	695	0.13

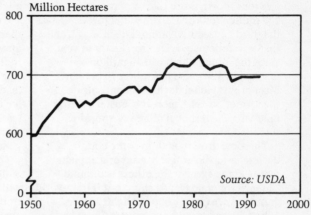

Figure 1: World Grain Harvested Area, 1950–92

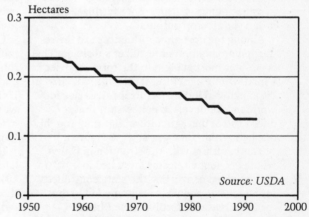

Figure 2: World Grain Harvested Area Per Person, 1950–92

SOURCE: USDA, *World Grain Database* (unpublished printouts) (Washington, D.C.: 1992); USDA, *World Grain Situation and Outlook*, Washington, D.C., April 1993.

Fertilizer Use Falls Again   Lester R. Brown

World fertilizer use in 1992 totalled 131 million tons, down more than 4 percent from the 137 million tons of 1991.[1] (See Figure 1.) It was the third consecutive annual decline, a trend that few anticipated. During the three years since the all-time high of 146 million tons reached in 1989, use has fallen 10 percent. Most of this global decline is concentrated in the former Soviet Union and Eastern Europe, following the removal of heavy subsidies there.[2]

The slow growth and, in some countries, decline in fertilizer use has several explanations—some agronomic, others economic. Three agronomic trends stand out. First, world grainland area has dropped slightly since 1981.[3] Second, growth in irrigated area has slowed dramatically since 1978, dropping to 1 percent a year.[4] And third, and perhaps most important, the response of crops to the additional use of fertilizer is diminishing.[5] Indeed, in some countries, using more fertilizer does little to boost crop output.

Among the economic influences are the reduction or abolition of fertilizer subsidies. This is perhaps most evident in the former Soviet Union, where agricultural reforms launched in 1988 included letting fertilizer prices rise to world market levels, a policy shift that reduced use of this agricultural input by roughly one half within four years.[6] (See Figure 2.)

This contrasts with the situation in China, where economic reforms launched in 1978 that involved converting the state-controlled farm sector to a market economy led to dramatic increases in fertilizer use.[7] In 1978, China's farmers were using 8.8 million tons of fertilizer. By 1992, this had climbed to 26.2 million tons, a threefold increase.[8]

Not surprisingly, there is a remarkable parallel between changes in the historical growth in world fertilizer use and grain output. From 1950 to 1984, world fertilizer use increased ninefold, from 14 million to 126 million tons, an annual rise of nearly 7 percent.[9] Then from 1984 to 1992 it grew less than 1 percent a year. For grain, the harvest went from 631 million tons in 1950 to 1,649 million tons in 1984, growing nearly 3 percent a year.[10] Since then, however, the rise in grain output has matched that of fertilizer use—less than 1 percent annually.

The four countries that account for more than half of world grain output—the United States, the former Soviet Union, China, and India—also account for half the fertilizer use.[11] The United States, traditionally the world leader in fertilizer use, was overtaken by the Soviet Union in the early eighties. The Soviet lead was short-lived, however, since by 1990 soaring fertilizer use in China had pushed that country to the top of the list.

Of the major food producers, the United States was the first in which fertilizer use levelled off. (See Figure 3.) After a rapid increase from 1950 through 1980, growth came to an abrupt halt. Since then usage has actually fallen somewhat, leading to lower fertilizer use in the early nineties than a decade earlier.[12] Some of the decline is due to more sophisticated tests that enable farmers to better match fertilizer applications to plant needs, thus eliminating the excessive use of fertilizer.

Of the big four grain producers, China has the smallest area of cropland, roughly two thirds as much as the United States and India and scarcely half that of the former Soviet Union.[13] Nonetheless, it has taken the lead in world fertilizer use because it has such a vast irrigated area, a key to the economic use of large amounts of fertilizer.

In India, fertilizer use climbed rapidly in the late eighties, largely as a result of heavy government subsidies. By the early nineties, though, opposition to this fiscal drain led to a reduction in subsidies and much slower growth in use.[14] Without subsidies, fertilizer use is likely to grow considerably more slowly in India in the years immediately ahead.

The trends of the last few years suggest that the era of rapid continuous growth in world fertilizer use, which lasted from mid-century to the mid-eighties, has come to an end. With the response of crop yields to additional applications of fertilizer diminishing, it is no longer clear where future gains in grain output will come from or whether they will be adequate.

WORLD FERTILIZER USE, 1950–92

YEAR	TOTAL (mill. tons)	PER CAPITA (kilograms)
1950	14	5.5
1951	15	5.8
1952	15	5.7
1953	16	6.0
1954	17	6.2
1955	18	6.5
1956	20	7.1
1957	22	7.6
1958	23	7.8
1959	25	8.3
1960	27	8.9
1961	28	9.1
1962	31	9.9
1963	34	10.6
1964	37	11.3
1965	40	12.0
1966	45	13.2
1967	51	14.6
1968	56	15.8
1969	60	16.5
1970	66	17.8
1971	69	18.2
1972	73	18.9
1973	79	20.1
1974	85	21.2
1975	82	20.1
1976	90	21.6
1977	95	22.5
1978	100	23.2
1979	111	25.3
1980	112	25.1
1981	117	25.8
1982	115	25.0
1983	115	24.5
1984	126	26.4
1985	131	27.0
1986	129	26.1
1987	132	26.3
1988	140	27.4
1989	146	28.0
1990	143	27.0
1991	137	25.4
1992 (prel)	131	23.9

SOURCES: FAO, *Fertilizer Yearbook 1991* (Rome: 1991); International Fertilizer Industry Association; Worldwatch Institute.

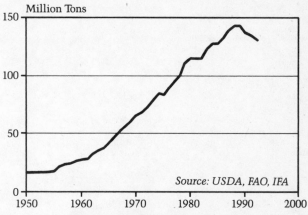

Figure 1: World Fertilizer Use, 1950–92

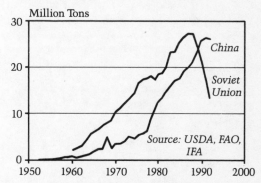

Figure 2: Fertilizer Use in China and the Soviet Union, 1950–92

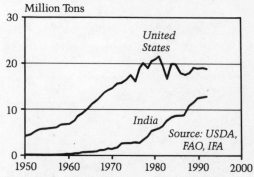

Figure 3: Fertilizer Use in the United States and India, 1950–92

Energy
Trends

Oil Production Steady
Christopher Flavin and Hal Kane

World oil production in 1992 remained even with its 1991 level of 58.8 million barrels per day, which was about 1 percent below the figure recorded in 1990.[1] (See Figure 1.) This levelling off is sparked in part by reduced demand stemming from the 1990–92 recession.

Global oil demand still lies well below the peak level of 1979. Improved energy efficiency and the expanding role of natural gas in many countries is cutting into petroleum's market. But oil is still the world's leading source of energy, supplying 40 percent of the total (excluding biomass).[2]

The former Soviet Union's oil output dropped 13.1 percent—1.3 million barrels a day—in 1992, continuing a recent plunge. (See Figure 2.) Use of oil in Russia also fell, however, allowing exports to remain steady.[3] U.S. oil production was cut 268,000 barrels a day, extending a decline under way since the mid-eighties.[4] Indonesia's oil production fell by 103,000 barrels per day in 1992, while Norway's production boomed—rising by 276,000 barrels a day.[5]

The Middle East continued to strengthen its dominance of the world oil market in 1992. The area's production rose 7.4 percent, equal to 1.2 million barrels a day, as Kuwait resumed much of its past production and as Iraq and the neutral zone between the two countries added output.[6] Overall, the Middle East controlled 27 percent of the world oil market in 1992, led by Saudi Arabia, which produced 8.1 million barrels per day and which retains the ability to raise or lower the world price of oil at will.[7]

Oil use was once expected to continue rising until resources were so depleted that production fell. But the high prices of the seventies led to a decline in demand that makes it unlikely production will ever reach the theoretical maximum level. Two factors now limit oil use: the willingness of the world to rely on the Middle East for supplies, and the environmental damage that stems from oil dependence.

The burning of oil emitted about 2.4 billion tons of carbon in 1992, accounting for more than 40 percent of total carbon emissions.[8] Among the other air pollutants it leads to are sulfur dioxide, nitrogen oxides, and hydrocarbons. Much of the oil is burned by motor vehicles, and the resulting pollutants are major contributors to urban smog.

Oil spills were also common in 1992. A tanker that ran aground near the Spanish coast lost a half-million barrels of crude oil, almost twice the amount spilled in the 1989 Exxon Valdez disaster.[9] A tanker collision near Indonesia dumped more than 200,000 barrels into the sea just four months after another ship in the same strait spilled 90,000 barrels.[10] And in early 1993, a wrecked tanker broke up against the rocky cliffs of the Shetland Islands, releasing more than a half-million barrels of crude oil.[11]

Pipeline accidents also occur frequently. In Russia, for example, a major pipeline break near the Siberian town of Uvat released more than 18,000 barrels of oil.[12] And a line gathering crude oil broke and ignited near Nizhnevartovsk.[13] Pipeline breaks in Russia and central Asia are described as "coming one after another."[14]

Efforts to improve energy efficiency may further slow the growth in oil demand in industrial countries during the nineties. Although the use of cars continues to grow rapidly in parts of Asia and Latin America, cities like Amsterdam and Mexico City have restricted the use of cars for environmental reasons.[15] And some analysts expect the growing use of compressed natural gas and biofuels, such as ethanol, to slowly eat into oil's dominance of the transportation fuels market.

Future oil trends will continue to be driven by demand rather than supply. In the near term, there is unlikely to be much demand growth due to further declines in oil use in Russia and Eastern Europe and relatively stagnant markets in industrial countries. Growth may resume in the late nineties, however—spurred by rising demand in the Far East and perhaps in Russia, if its economic decline is reversed. Nevertheless, efficiency, natural gas, and renewables will continue to chip away at oil's markets.

WORLD OIL PRODUCTION, 1950–92

YEAR	PRODUCTION (mill. barrels per day)
1950	10.4
1951	11.7
1952	12.4
1953	13.2
1954	13.7
1955	15.4
1956	16.8
1957	17.6
1958	18.1
1959	19.5
1960	21.0
1961	22.4
1962	24.3
1963	26.1
1964	28.2
1965	30.3
1966	32.9
1967	35.4
1968	38.8
1969	41.7
1970	45.8
1971	48.4
1972	51.0
1973	55.8
1974	56.3
1975	53.4
1976	58.1
1977	60.0
1978	60.7
1979	62.7
1980	59.6
1981	55.8
1982	53.1
1983	52.6
1984	54.1
1985	53.4
1986	55.7
1987	55.3
1988	57.7
1989	58.6
1990	59.5
1991	58.8
1992 (prel)	58.8

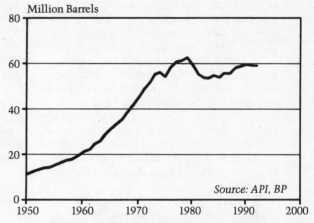

Figure 1: World Oil Production Per Day, 1950–92

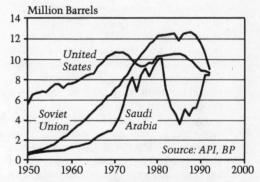

Figure 2: U.S., Soviet, and Saudi Arabian Oil Production Per Day, 1950–92

SOURCES: American Petroleum Institute (API), *Basic Petroleum Data Book* (Washington, D.C.: 1992); 1991 figure from API, private communication, March 29, 1993; 1992 figure is Worldwatch Institute estimate based on *Oil & Gas Journal,* March 8, 1993.

Wind Generating Capacity Expands   Lester R. Brown

In 1992, the world's wind power generating capacity reached 2,652 megawatts, up from 2,347 megawatts in 1991.[1] (See Figure 1.) This annual growth of 13 percent makes wind one of the world's fastest growing energy sources.[2]

Starting in 1981 at a modest 15 megawatts, wind generating capacity grew rapidly during the mid and late eighties, with the surge concentrated in California. By the early nineties, most of the growth occurred in Europe as several governments there actively encouraged investment in wind energy.[3] Even so, as 1992 ended, the United States had 1,723 megawatts of capacity to Europe's 862 megawatts.[4] (See Figure 2.)

The world's wind electric generating potential is enormous. In Europe, wind power could theoretically satisfy all the continent's electricity needs.[5] In the United States, the wind-rich Great Plains alone could in theory meet the nation's electricity needs several times over.[6]

Recent advances in wind machine designs that boost efficiency allow turbines to operate at slower speeds, and thus increase the wind power potential that can be economically harvested.[7] Constraints on siting, particularly in densely populated regions, also reduce the potential for harnessing wind energy well below the theoretical maximum.

The largest share of electricity generated by wind energy is found in Denmark, where wind turbines, widely distributed over the countryside, are expected to meet 3 percent of electricity needs in 1993.[8] The modern wind energy industry began there in the late seventies, followed by major gains in California during the early eighties. The adoption by California of a state tax credit on investment in renewable energy resources in addition to an existing federal tax credit and favorable utility contracts created an attractive environment for investments in renewable energy resources.[9] With this stimulus, California emerged as the world leader in wind electric generation.

The United States could lose this lead. The European Community has adopted an official goal for 2005 of getting 8,000 megawatts of electric generating capacity from wind, enough to satisfy 1 percent of its electricity needs.[10] Within this framework, Denmark, Germany, and the Netherlands have each set national goals of developing at least 1,000 megawatts of wind generating capacity by the target date.[11] Southern Europe is also beginning to show an interest. Spain, for example, plans to install 200 megawatts of wind generating turbines on the wind-swept hills overlooking Gibraltar.[12]

Still under negotiation is an agreement between U.S. Windpower, a Ukrainian utility, and a Ukrainian manufacturer to build a 500-megawatt wind farm to help close down one of the Chernobyl nuclear reactors.[13] This is but one example of how governments throughout the world are discovering the enormous potential for wind electric generation. Other areas rich in wind energy include western China, parts of India, northwest Brazil, the Andean regions of Latin America, and North Africa.

Growth prospects in the United States are now brightening because of three recent government initiatives. The first was the National Energy Policy Act passed in late 1992, which provides a tax credit of 1.5¢ per kilowatt-hour of electricity generated from wind.[14] The second is the energy tax proposed by President Clinton in February 1993, which exempts both wind and solar energy.[15] These tax advantages, combined with the stringent air pollution controls of the Clean Air Act that will take effect in the second half of this decade, further strengthen the incentive to invest in U.S. wind generating capacity. Already plans exist for new wind farms in Iowa, Maine, Minnesota, and Washington.[16]

Wind energy is environmentally attractive for many reasons. It produces no health-damaging air pollution, forest-destroying acid rain, climate-destabilizing carbon emissions, or dangerous radioactive waste. Its principal drawback is that some consider it to be a visual pollutant.

With the harnessing of this new energy source scheduled to grow rapidly during the nineties, the international race to gain the lead in wind turbine design and manufacturing is under way.

WORLD WIND ENERGY
GENERATING CAPACITY, 1981–92

YEAR	CAPACITY (megawatts)
1981	15
1982	80
1983	260
1984	657
1985	971
1986	1,325
1987	1,419
1988	1,385
1989	1,636
1990	1,961
1991	2,347
1992 (prel)	2,652

SOURCE: Paul Gipe, American Wind Energy
Association, Tehachapi, calif., private
communication, March 30, 1993.

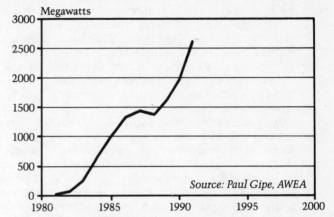

Source: Paul Gipe, AWEA

Figure 1: World Wind Energy Generating Capacity, 1981–92

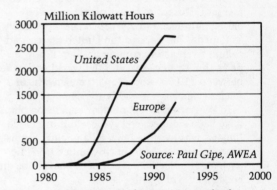

Source: Paul Gipe, AWEA

**Figure 2: Wind Energy Generation in
United States and Europe, 1981–92**

Nuclear Power at Virtual Standstill   Nicholas Lenssen

Between the end of 1991 and 1992, total installed nuclear generating capacity increased slightly, going from 326,000 megawatts to 328,000 megawatts.[1] (See Figure 1.) The figure remains, however, below the historical high of 329,000 megawatts reached in 1990. Given the decrease in plants under construction and the increase in plant closings, worldwide nuclear capacity could soon peak.

Forty-five nuclear plants (with a combined capacity of 38,000 megawatts) are under active construction worldwide, the fewest in a quarter-century.[2] Most of these are scheduled to be completed in the next three years.

Some 79 reactors, with a total generating capacity of 19,000 megawatts, have already been retired, after an average service life of less than 17 years.[3] (See Figure 2.) As technical problems in older reactors continue to crop up, the annual number of retirements is likely to increase. Dozens of larger plants could be closed in the next few years in countries such as Canada, Russia, and the United States, cancelling out reactors coming on-line. It now appears that by decade's end the world will have between 310,000 and 335,000 megawatts of nuclear capacity—roughly the same as now.[4]

In Western Europe, nuclear expansion plans have been stopped everywhere but in France. Finland was expected to lead a nuclear renaissance in Europe—but in November 1992 the parliament rejected government plans to begin construction of a fifth plant.[5]

Even the vaunted French nuclear program is now in jeopardy. Only five plants are under construction, and just two have been started since 1986. The standardization of French plants carries the inherent risk of widespread generic faults. Growing technical problems have led to extensive maintenance and repairs, costing billions of francs. And steam generators and reactor vessel heads will have to be replaced at most plants.[6]

In the United States, Bill Clinton is the first president in the last half-century who does not favor building more plants. Just two reactors are under active construction; it has been 20 years since a reactor order was placed there that was not subsequently cancelled.[7] Meanwhile, six aging reactors with a combined capacity of 3,695 megawatts have been permanently closed in the past four years.

In Canada, the state-owned utility Ontario Hydro planned on completing 10 more reactors by 2014.[8] But provincial elections in September 1990—and the realization that Ontario Hydro's power already cost far more than the electricity that independent producers could provide—led to cancellation of the expansion program. The company is now considering early retirement for some older, problem-plagued reactors in need of repair.[9]

Nuclear programs in the former East Bloc are in disarray. Democracy and a post-Chernobyl epidemic in radiation-induced thyroid cancer in children unleashed a torrent of public criticism focusing on the failure of nuclear plants to meet western safety standards.[10] Western nations have called for the closure of some two dozen older, unsafe reactors, a call not yet heeded. Meanwhile, scores of nuclear plants have been cancelled or mothballed in Bulgaria, the former Czechoslovakia, Hungary, Poland, Russia, and Ukraine.[11] Just three reactors remain under construction in the former Soviet Union—far below the 20 planned by the Russian government as of December 1992.[12]

East Asia accounts for nearly 40 percent of the plants still being built. But there, too, public opposition is rising and utilities are considering alternatives. Japan still has an active nuclear construction program, despite a spate of recent accidents and the worldwide outcry over its policy to import processed plutonium from France.[13] South Korea has five reactors currently being built and aims to add some 18 more over the next 13 years—at an expected cost nearly double that of existing plants.[14] And Taiwan appears set to resume a project delayed for over 10 years.[15] In all three countries, though, expansion plans are far more modest than those of a decade earlier.[16]

As utilities begin to close commercial reactors, it has become clear that the real cost of dismantling retired nuclear power plants may rival the cost of building them.[17] For companies still thinking about putting up new ones, this is a large and unplanned liability that will further discourage nuclear construction plans.

WORLD NET INSTALLED ELECTRICAL
GENERATING CAPACITY OF
NUCLEAR POWER PLANTS, 1954–92

YEAR	CAPACITY
	(megawatts)
1954	5
1955	5
1956	50
1957	100
1958	190
1959	380
1960	830
1961	850
1962	1,800
1963	2,100
1964	3,100
1965	4,800
1966	6,200
1967	8,300
1968	9,200
1969	13,000
1970	16,000
1971	24,000
1972	32,000
1973	45,000
1974	61,000
1975	71,000
1976	85,000
1977	99,000
1978	114,000
1979	121,000
1980	135,000
1981	155,000
1982	170,000
1983	189,000
1984	219,000
1985	250,000
1986	276,000
1987	297,000
1988	311,000
1989	321,000
1990	329,000
1991	326,000
1992 (prel)	328,000

SOURCES: Worldwatch Institute data base, compiled
from the International Atomic Energy Agency and
press reports.

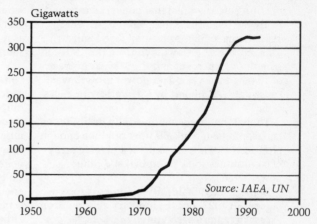

**Figure 1: World Electrical Generating Capacity
of Nuclear Power Plants, 1950–92**

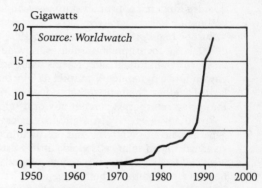

**Figure 2: Cumulative Nuclear Generating
Capacity Decommissioned, 1964–92**

Photovoltaic Sales Growth Slows   Hal Kane

World shipments of photovoltaic (PV) cells, the thin silicon wafers that convert sunlight directly into electricity, increased 5 percent in 1992, rising to 58 megawatts.[1] (See Figure 1.) This represents a slowdown from the 1991 growth of 19 percent and the 10-year average of 15 percent a year. The slower growth was caused at least in part by the worldwide recession.[2]

Though not used commercially until the seventies, photovoltaic cells now produce enough electricity worldwide to meet a diverse array of communications, pumping, and other power needs.

In the United States, PV shipments rose 6 percent in 1992, but the industry suffered from excess inventories, saturated markets, lack of government support, and the recession. The biggest drop in sales, a 6-percent decline, came in Japan, as its first economic decline in decades hindered consumer purchases and investment.[3]

European orders rose 22 percent in 1992, due to large government purchases, new subsidies, growth in foreign aid projects using solar power, and a dynamic PV market in Switzerland. Together, the United States, Japan, and Europe account for 92 percent of world sales.[4]

Producing electricity from photovoltaics generates no air pollution. And production of standard silicon solar cells yields little waste. New cell technologies are being developed, however, and some of them do generate some toxic materials. Large-scale production of some multilayer cells that use exotic materials like gallium arsenide or cadmium sulfide also produces some toxins.[5]

Solar panels take up considerable space. Compared with other sources of energy, however, their use of land is not excessive. Coal, for example, needs more land than solar power does if the area devoted to mining is included.[6] Moreover, solar panels can sit on rooftops, along highways, and in sun-rich but otherwise empty deserts.

PV cells have a versatility that allows them to be placed in remote locations and a modular construction that makes them easy to transport and relocate. As a result, they often supply electricity to rural areas and remote locations less expensively than central power plants would. And, of course, the sunshine they convert into electricity is more widely distributed around the globe than any other energy source.

Villagers in remote regions are using photovoltaic cells for lighting, radios, and household needs. More than 60,000 photovoltaic lighting units have been installed in recent years in developing countries such as Colombia, the Dominican Republic, Mexico, and Sri Lanka; Kenya has 10 private companies selling photovoltaics, with as much as 1,000 kilowatts installed.[7] Photovoltaic power can be more cost-effective for people in rural areas than diesel generators or other available alternatives. Other practical applications include rural health and immunization facilities and water pumping.[8]

Most governments, however, have failed to exploit the potential of solar cells. Research and development (R&D) funding by industrial countries of all kinds of solar power totalled $289 million in 1991, compared with $989 million spent on coal and $4.49 billion for nuclear reactors.[9] Solar power amounted to 3.5 percent of total R&D funds.[10] Some European governments are now increasing their support for PVs, however. Spain, for example, put over 17 percent of its energy R&D into solar, Germany put 16 percent, and Switzerland, 14 percent.[11] In the United States, government funding for solar energy fell 80 percent in the eighties, although budgets are now rising again.[12]

The main obstacle to the proliferation of PV technology is price. In the future, costs are likely to fall with continuing efforts to develop more-efficient, cheaper technologies. But solar electric power still costs $4.50 per watt of new generating capacity (resulting in a price of more than 30¢ per kilowatt-hour, about six times as much as fossil-fuel-based electricity).[13] (See Figure 2.) Once its price approaches the cost of producing electricity from fossil fuels, photovoltaics can be expected to proliferate.

WORLD PHOTOVOLTAIC SHIPMENTS, 1971–92

YEAR	SHIPMENTS (megawatts)
1971	0.1
1975	1.8
1976	2.0
1977	2.2
1978	2.5
1979	4.0
1980	6.5
1981	7.8
1982	9.1
1983	21.7
1984	25.0
1985	22.8
1986	26.0
1987	29.2
1988	33.8
1989	40.2
1990	46.5
1991	55.3
1992 (prel)	57.9

SOURCE: Paul Maycock, *PV News,* February 1992, February 1985, and February 1982.

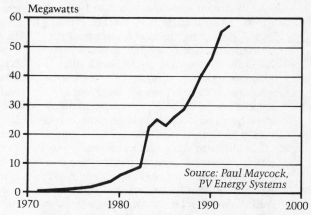

Figure 1: World Photovoltaic Shipments, 1971–92

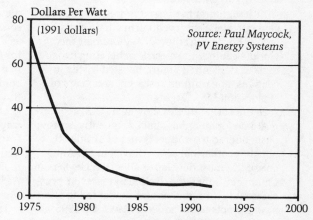

Figure 2: Average Factory Prices for Photovoltaic Modules, 1975–92

Worldwide geothermal electrical generating capacity passed 9,369 megawatts in 1991, up from 8,777 megawatts in 1990.[1] (See Figure 1.) This tapping of hot fluids and gases beneath the earth's surface now offers as much power as 6 million Americans use.[2] Though still minor compared with fossil fuels, geothermal power nevertheless offers some regions a major source of carbon-free energy. In many areas, however, it poses environmental problems of its own.

In addition to using geothermal energy to generate electricity, many countries use it directly in factories or to heat water and buildings without ever turning it into electricity. In 1990, global direct use reached the equivalent of 11,730 megawatts. Almost a quarter of that was in Japan. China had 2,140 megawatts, up from only 390 in 1985. And Hungary had 1,280 megawatts, closely followed by the former Soviet Union, with 1,130.[3]

Although first harnessed in Italy in 1904 to generate electricity, geothermal has found its largest home in California.[4] About half the world's geothermal electric generating capacity is in the United States, boosted by tax incentives, government research, and years of exploration.[5] (See Figure 2.)

In the early nineties, however, U.S. geothermal development has slowed. Incentives previously offered to producers and to utilities that bought geothermal power have ended. And one of the most developed sites, the Geysers in California, suffered a decline in reservoir pressures and steam deliverability that led to all new projects being halted in 1989. By 1995, only another 400 megawatts of geothermal power are expected to be added in the United States.[6] That would be an increase of about 15 percent, compared with a 90-percent increase between 1985 and 1989.

The Philippines has the second largest capacity, with geothermal providing 15 percent of its electricity in 1990, and an expected 30 percent by decade's end.[7] This would make the Philippines the world's largest geothermal producer.[8] (See Figure 2.) But it would require the construction of a plant on Mount Apo, which is sacred to several tribes, as well as the clearing of some virgin forests. And it would threaten several species, including the endangered Philippine eagle.[9]

Mexico is the third largest generator, with 12 percent of the world's geothermal electric capacity, and Italy is fourth, at 9 percent.[10] Japan, with 65 volcanoes and many geothermal fields, has as an estimated 69,000 megawatts of potential. It hopes to reach 1,000 megawatts of output by the year 2000.[11] In Iceland, geothermal accounts for a third of total energy consumption and provides most space heating and hot water.[12]

Electricity produced from the earth's heat typically costs 4.5–6¢ per kilowatt-hour,[13] although different sites produce at widely varying prices, compared with 5–7¢ for fossil-fuel-based electricity.[14] Geothermal is more reliable than other renewable sources because it is not intermittent. And like other renewables, it emits few pollutants and little or no carbon.

Although geothermal reserves can be depleted if not managed correctly, worldwide resources are sufficiently large for it to be treated as a renewable resource. In the United States, for example, the Department of Energy estimates that hydrothermal reservoirs alone could produce 2,400 quads of energy—30 times current annual U.S. energy use.[15] (Most geothermal plants draw hot water or steam trapped in gaps in the rock at depths ranging from 100 meters to about 3 kilometers; classified as "hydrothermal" energy, this is the most common type of geothermal operation.) As long as reserves are managed carefully, there is little danger of running out.

In the future, two other geothermal resources may be tapped. The first is abundant "geopressured" energy—dissolved methane trapped at depths of 3–6 kilometers. Still more difficult to obtain is energy from hot dry rock that does not have liquid around it.[16] The resource is huge, but ways must be found to fracture the rock, inject water, and then recover it. Considerable research needs to be done before such techniques stand a chance of becoming economical. Even without those new techniques, however, world geothermal power is projected to grow at about 10 percent a year in the mid-nineties.

WORLD GEOTHERMAL ELECTRICAL
GENERATING CAPACITY, 1950–91

YEAR	CAPACITY (megawatts)
1950	239
1951	239
1952	239
1953	242
1954	242
1955	246
1956	246
1957	265
1958	362
1959	362
1960	368
1961	413
1962	487
1963	550
1964	550
1965	558
1966	561
1967	650
1968	679
1969	704
1970	715
1971	834
1972	941
1973	1,150
1974	1,167
1975	1,314
1976	1,314
1977	1,314
1978	1,390
1979	1,896
1980	2,390
1981	2,422
1982	2,822
1983	3,383
1984	4,164
1985	5,954
1986	6,505
1987	7,098
1988	7,279
1989	8,095
1990	8,777
1991	9,369

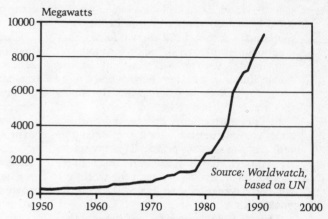

Figure 1: World Geothermal Electric Generating Capacity, 1950–91

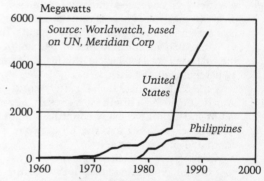

Figure 2: U.S. and Philippine Geothermal Electric Generating Capacity, 1960–91

SOURCE: United Nations, Department of International Economic and Social Affairs, *Energy Statistics Yearbook* (New York: various years);1991 data from Energy Office, United Nations, New York, private communication, April 23, 1993.

Coal Use Growth Ends

Christopher Flavin and Hal Kane

After four decades of nearly uninterrupted growth, world use of coal is no longer growing. It fell 1.4 percent during 1990 and 1991, and preliminary data for 1992 show it falling another 0.3 percent, to 2.18 billion tons (oil equivalent).[1] (See Figure 1.) Economic contraction in Russia and Eastern Europe and a more modest recession elsewhere primarily caused the drop.

In nineteenth century Europe and North America, coal fueled the Industrial Revolution, replacing wood as the principal energy source. Even though oil overtook it early this century, coal still provides 28 percent of the world's commercial energy.[2] And its use has more than doubled since 1950.[3]

Though coal was once burned directly to heat homes and to power the steam engines in trains and machinery, most of those markets have since been taken by oil, natural gas, or electricity. In advanced industrial countries, only two major uses of coal remain: smelting iron ore and running electric power plants. In the United States, for example, 87 percent of the coal used goes to electric utilities, up from 17 percent in 1949.[4]

While coal lost market share after World War II, it enjoyed a brief resurgence in the seventies and eighties as many countries sought to replace increasingly expensive oil with a more affordable energy source.

More recently, coal has come under pressure from mounting evidence of the environmental damage it causes. Strip mining has laid waste to hundreds of square kilometers in some countries, while coal mining has left miners with black lung disease and filled drinking water with hazardous chemicals. And burning coal emits huge quantities of sulfur and nitrogen oxides, which are damaging crops and forests in scores of countries.[5]

New pollution control technologies can help alleviate some of these problems, but not coal's threat to the global climate. Coal contains 80 percent more carbon per unit of energy than natural gas does and 30 percent more than oil. Burning it released 2.4 billion tons of carbon into the atmosphere in 1990, and trapping the carbon that coal releases would be expensive, probably prohibitively

so.[6] Some governments are addressing this issue by levying carbon taxes that make coal more expensive and discourage its use.

Global coal use appears likely to plateau and then begin falling in the decades ahead as governments cut subsidies and tighten environmental laws. Over time, the need to meet environmental standards will hurt coal's competitiveness against other fuels.

Many governments maintain coal subsidies to protect mineworkers' jobs. In Germany, for example, coal prices are held at more than five times the world market level.[7] The U.K. government tried to eliminate subsidies and shut down much of the state-controlled coal industry in 1992, but was forced by mineworkers to delay its plans.[8] Two other major producers—China and Poland—each laid off 100,000 miners in 1992 and announced plans to go much further in the future.[9]

Coal mining jobs are also being lost because of the move to strip mining, which is more efficient, as well as the switch to cleaner fuels. In the United States, for instance, coal production rose 15 percent from 1980 to 1988, but mining jobs fell 40 percent.[10]

Coal's last bastion is in a handful of developing countries that cannot afford heavy use of oil and still use coal everywhere, including in the home. China, for example, is now the leading consumer of this fossil fuel (see Figures 2 and 3), with one quarter of the world total, while India ranks fourth.[11] China currently gets 75 percent of its energy from coal—similar to Britain in the nineteenth century—and planners envision a 40-percent increase in the next eight years. Extensive lung and crop damage tied to the country's heavy dependence on coal are now threatening those plans, however.[12]

Meanwhile, coal use is already falling quickly in the former Soviet Union, where it dropped 18 percent from 1988 to 1991.[13] Further declines are likely as Russia and other republics shut down inefficient coal-fueled factories and replace them with more-efficient plants that run on natural gas.

WORLD COAL CONSUMPTION, 1950–91

YEAR	CONSUMPTION (mill. tons of oil equivalent)
1950	1,028
1951	1,101
1952	1,097
1953	1,111
1954	1,117
1955	1,215
1956	1,262
1957	1,288
1958	1,337
1959	1,385
1960	1,478
1961	1,365
1962	1,394
1963	1,455
1964	1,489
1965	1,465
1966	1,489
1967	1,428
1968	1,493
1969	1,522
1970	1,543
1971	1,533
1972	1,530
1973	1,557
1974	1,574
1975	1,599
1976	1,667
1977	1,712
1978	1,734
1979	1,828
1980	1,814
1981	1,816
1982	1,846
1983	1,892
1984	1,971
1985	2,049
1986	2,091
1987	2,153
1988	2,202
1989	2,218
1990	2,201
1991	2,186
1992 (prel)	2,180

SOURCE:: United Nations, *Energy Statistics Yearbooks* (various years); British Petroleum, London, computer printout of historical data; Worldwatch Institute.

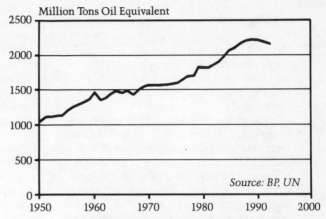

Million Tons Oil Equivalent

Source: BP, UN

Figure 1: World Coal Consumption, 1950–92

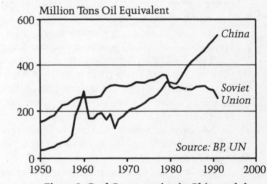

Million Tons Oil Equivalent

China

Soviet Union

Source: BP, UN

Figure 2: Coal Consumption in China and the Soviet Union, 1950–91

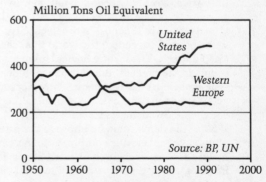

Million Tons Oil Equivalent

United States

Western Europe

Source: BP, UN

Figure 3: Coal Consumption in the United States and Western Europe, 1950–91

Hydroelectric Power Growth Steady   Hal Kane

In 1991, the world continued to add to its capacity to generate electricity from the motion of falling river water, reaching 644,000 megawatts—a 2.4-percent increase over 1990.[1] (See Figure 1.) That figure has risen more than fourteenfold since 1950.[2] Today's largest renewable source of electricity, hydroelectric power provides more than 20 percent of the world's electricity.[3]

Hydropower emits no carbon dioxide and little pollution, though it destroys land and water habitats and causes erosion of soils and silting of rivers. It originates in the energy from the sun that powers the hydrological cycle. Rain and snow deposited at higher elevations represent a vast storage of potential energy that can be harnessed as it makes its way to the sea. Most of the hydropower potential lies in mountainous regions that are often pristine and biologically diverse.[4]

This renewable energy technology predates fossil fuels, though new, more-efficient designs continue to yield improvements. Its costs are competitive with fossil fuels in many situations, although its growth potential is limited by the availability of suitable river sites. About one quarter of the world's hydropower potential has been exploited, and it is unlikely that all of it ever will be, due to environmental and social constraints.[5]

Hydropower is important in many developing countries, which generate 37 percent of the world's total.[6] And some regions, such as central Africa, have only begun to tap their hydro capacity. Worldwide, the United States and Canada produce the most hydroelectricity, with about 13 percent of the world total each. (See Figure 2.) The former Soviet Union accounts for 10 percent, Brazil produces 9 percent, and China has 5 percent.[7] Tiny Norway gets 95 percent of its electricity from falling water, and Sweden gets roughly half.[8]

Some old dams could be improved or fitted with power-generating equipment to increase hydroelectric power. In the United States, for instance, fewer than 3 percent of the 67,000 existing dams currently produce electricity. They were built for flood control but could be adapted to generate electricity, often for less than the cost of new coal or oil plants.[9] The U.S. Department of Energy estimates that up to 10,000 megawatts of potential small-scale hydropower could be developed.[10] But those changes would reduce fish populations, disrupt water flows, and flood land.

Some older hydro plants whose initial investments have already been amortized produce power at less than 1¢ per kilowatt-hour, a small fraction of the cost of other methods.[11] But many new projects are quite expensive, and the large initial investment required often discourages hydroelectric development, particularly in developing countries.

In some hydro projects, a technology called pumped hydro lifts water to high reservoirs, so that electricity will be generated when the water is released back down. The purpose is to store the energy until it is needed. The water can be pumped up high at night, or during off-hours, and then released during times of peak demand. In the United States, for instance, the flexible generating schedules that pumped hydro makes possible have inspired the initiation of five new projects that would add at least 5,300 megawatts of energy storage capacity during the nineties.[12]

Major refurbishment of most hydro plants is not required for 30–50 years, and with proper upkeep they can last for centuries.[13] But many dams have been built without adequate environmental or social research. Some have had to be rebuilt or abandoned because deforestation and soil erosion quickly filled reservoirs with silt and made them useless. Other projects have flooded so much agricultural land, displaced so many people, or caused such extensive water pollution that their negative effects have outweighed positive ones.

Opposition to hydropower is increasingly strong in the cases of the dams that are displacing the most people or flooding the most land. The Three Gorges dam under construction in China will displace more than a million people.[14] And the Narmada river dams in India will require far more people to move, with some estimates over 10 million.[15] So although hydro generating capacity will continue to be added to the world total, rapid increases are unlikely.

WORLD HYDROELECTRIC GENERATING CAPACITY, 1950–91

YEAR	CAPACITY (megawatts)
1950	44,596
1951	47,577
1952	51,326
1953	56,698
1954	61,817
1955	67,857
1956	114,916
1957	125,211
1958	135,106
1959	145,450
1960	157,080
1961	168,588
1962	180,206
1963	192,997
1964	203,028
1965	214,023
1966	223,997
1967	236,088
1968	251,249
1969	266,900
1970	282,491
1971	295,564
1972	305,339
1973	324,767
1974	339,271
1975	366,458
1976	383,667
1977	396,426
1978	408,569
1979	443,836
1980	466,938
1981	483,938
1982	505,041
1983	517,899
1984	538,429
1985	555,463
1986	574,275
1987	584,977
1988	608,674
1989	622,058
1990	628,429
1991 (prel)	643,511

SOURCE: United Nations, Department of International Economic and Social Affairs, *Energy Statistics Yearbook* (New York: various years); British Petroleum, *BP Statistical Review of World Energy* (London: 1992).

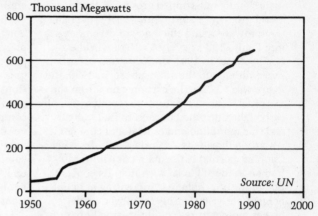

Figure 1: World Hydroelectric Generating Capacity, 1950–91

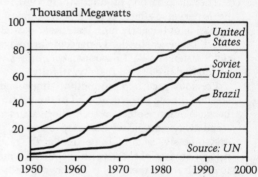

Figure 2: Hydroelectric Generating Capacity, United States, Soviet Union, and Brazil, 1950–91

Carbon Efficiency Down Slightly   C. Flavin and H. Kane

Growth in global carbon emissions from fossil fuels slightly outstripped growth in the gross world product in 1991, temporarily reversing a trend toward rising efficiency of carbon use. (See Figure 1.) For every $3.19 of world economic output in 1991, one kilogram of carbon was emitted into the atmosphere; in 1990, the figure was $3.22.[1] The carbon came from the use of oil, coal, and natural gas, which give off carbon dioxide when burned to fuel industry and transportation and to heat and cool homes.

Carbon dioxide is a colorless, odorless, heat-trapping gas that is the main contributor to human-induced global warming. Its concentration in the atmosphere is increasing at half a percent per year. During the next decade, higher temperatures could threaten both crop and forest productivity.[2]

The fall in carbon productivity in 1991 reflects perverse effects of the global economic recession of the early nineties. It was partially offset, however, by the 17-percent shrinkage of the Russian and East European economies, which had used fossil fuels wastefully.[3]

Previously, carbon productivity improved steadily during the second half of the century because of more-efficient technologies and a trend away from heavy industry to less energy-intensive sectors. In particular, the oil price increases of the seventies spurred a move toward improved energy efficiency. In addition, a trend toward products that consume little energy, such as educational services, telecommunications, and entertainment, has tended to reduce carbon emissions.

In recent years, carbon emissions in North America and Western Europe have remained nearly steady, while economic growth averaged 2–3 percent per year.[4] (See Figure 2.) Energy use in industrial countries grew only one fifth as much as their economies between the first oil shock of 1973 and 1989.[5]

Shifting to new energy sources can also lower carbon emissions: burning coal creates the greatest amount of carbon; oil is second; and natural gas third. So an economy that shifts to natural gas will put less carbon into the air; one that depends on coal will put out much more. Using renewable sources of energy (such as solar, wind, and hydroelectric power) or nuclear power, on the other hand, emits no carbon.

The dramatic gains that are possible in carbon productivity are evident in a simple example. Shifting from a conventional coal-fired power plant to a new combined-cycle natural-gas-fueled power plant reduces carbon emissions by 60 percent.[6] If the electricity coming from that plant is then used in an efficient compact fluorescent lamp rather than a conventional light bulb, the electricity used for lighting is also reduced—by 75 percent.[7] The combined result: one tenth as much carbon is emitted to produce the same amount of light—a 90-percent reduction in carbon emissions.

Until recently, carbon efficiency was higher in developing countries than industrial ones because the poor countries had less energy-intensive economies. But between 1973 and 1989, energy use in developing countries expanded 20 percent faster than economic output.[8] Developing countries now produce less gross national product per kilogram of carbon emissions than industrial countries do. They are in an energy-intensive phase of development. And as less-efficient technologies cost less up front, cash-strapped countries tend to rely on them.

Since energy users do not pay for the pollution they emit, they have little reason to maximize their carbon productivity. For example, the true cost of driving a car is much higher than the cost of gasoline if the damage done by carbon emissions and other pollutants is included. William Cline of the Institute for International Economics estimates the annual costs to the U.S. economy from global warming, assuming a doubling of carbon concentrations in the atmosphere, at about $60 billion toward the middle of the next century.[9]

At the Earth Summit in 1992, most industrial countries and many developing ones—154 countries in all—signed a global climate treaty that is designed to limit carbon emissions.[10] Although the treaty does not include any specific national goals, many governments have already adopted their own targets and timetables.

CARBON EFFICIENCY OF THE WORLD ECONOMY, 1950–91

YEAR	EFFICIENCY (dollars GWP per kilogram emitted)
1950	2.35
1955	2.43
1960	2.40
1961	2.50
1962	2.52
1963	2.50
1964	2.53
1965	2.55
1966	2.55
1967	2.56
1968	2.58
1969	2.60
1970	2.52
1971	2.53
1972	2.55
1973	2.57
1974	2.59
1975	2.62
1976	2.61
1977	2.64
1978	2.72
1979	2.67
1980	2.74
1981	2.86
1982	2.90
1983	2.98
1984	3.01
1985	3.05
1986	3.03
1987	3.08
1988	3.10
1989	3.16
1990	3.22
1991 (prel)	3.19

SOURCES: Thomas A. Boden et al., *Trends '91: A Compendium of Data on Global Change* (Oak Ridge, Tenn.: ORNL, 1991); British Petroleum, *BP Statistical Review of World Energy* (London: 1992); World Bank and IMF; gross world product data for 1950 and 1955 from Herbert R. Block, *The Planetary Product in 1980: A Creative Pause?* (Washington, D.C.: U.S. Department of State, 1981).

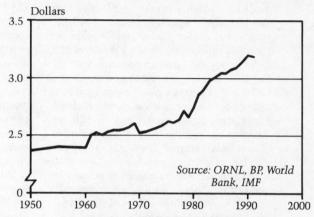

Figure 1: World Economic Output Per Kilogram of Carbon Emitted, 1950-91

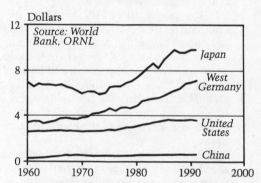

Figure 2: Economic Output Per Kilogram of Carbon Emitted, Japan, West Germany, United States, and China, 1960–91

Compact Fluorescents Catching On   David Malin Roodman

Worldwide sales of the compact fluorescent lamp (CFL)—a highly efficient replacement for regular household light bulbs—increased 23 percent in 1992.[1] (See Figure 1.) Sales that year reached 134 million, triple the 1988 level of 45 million.[2] By replacing incandescents, the CFLs sold in 1992 alone will cut demand for electricity by up to 6,000 megawatts, equivalent to the output of about seven nuclear power plants.[3]

In terms of sales volume, CFLs are still easily dwarfed by the roughly 9 billion incandescents purchased around the world each year.[4] But the lamps last long enough that on average each one supplants a succession of at least 10 regular bulbs. Thus while CFLs accounted for less than 2 percent of the lamps of their size sold in 1992, they had actually captured a 13-percent market share in terms of hours of lighting capacity sold.

CFLs represented a $2-billion market in 1992, one quarter of the total market for regular household lights in dollar terms.[5] Western Europe accounted for 44 percent of the sales; North America, for 28 percent; and Japan, for 13 percent.[6] (See Figure 2.) In the West European countries where the CFL is strongest, sales of regular bulbs have stagnated, apparently as a direct result of the competition from CFLs.

The classic incandescent bulb is inefficient and short-lived because more than 90 percent of the energy it draws goes to heating a filament enough for it to glow—in essence, burning it up over time.[7] In contrast, the CFL uses electricity to excite a tube-confined gas, which then radiates ultraviolet rays. Phosphors on the inner surface of the tube convert the radiation to visible light. This results in a lamp with four times the efficiency of a standard bulb, and 10 times the longevity.[8]

Although the CFL's price, at $15–20 per bulb, discourages most consumers, its efficiency and longevity more than cover this expense in most situations. For example, once bought, a CFL consuming electricity at 8¢ per kilowatt-hour (an average U.S. rate) for three hours each day will eventually save the buyer $35, even accounting for the lost income from not putting the money into long-term savings. In Japan, where electricity costs more than 13¢ per kilowatt-hour, the same CFL would save $55.[9]

Because of the high initial price, most of the consumer demand for CFLs has developed in regions where utilities or government agencies have directly sought to encourage it, usually through rebates and consumer education. In some West European countries, these programs are part of larger government efforts to reduce carbon emissions. In the United States, many electric utilities have pursued investments in efficiency primarily as a cost-effective alternative to new power plant construction.

Wherever the new lamp has caught on, it has saved money for both utilities and ratepayers by slowing the growth of expenditures on electric power plant construction and operation. And by requiring less electricity from traditional sources—nuclear energy, hydropower, and fossil fuels—the CFL helps reduce environmental problems, including radioactive waste generation, thermal pollution, the damming of rivers, acid rain, and global warming. In the United States, full conversion to CFLs would cut electricity use in homes up to 8 percent, which would shave 1 percent off total energy use.[10]

The potential gain from accelerating the shift to CFLs is even greater in developing countries, where demand for electricity is growing fastest and where much of the energy infrastructure is still being planned and built. Currently, a handful of these countries manufacture CFLs, but mostly for export to industrial countries. A few, however—notably Brazil and China—are currently producing large numbers for domestic use.[11] By lessening the need for new electrical generating capacity, these countries free up precious financial resources for more productive purposes.

SALES OF COMPACT
FLUORESCENT BULBS, TOTAL,
WESTERN EUROPE, AND
NORTH AMERICA, 1988–92

YEAR	WORLD (million)
1988	45
1989	59
1990	82
1991	109
1992	134

YEAR	WESTERN EUROPE
1988	24
1989	30
1990	40
1991	49
1992	59

YEAR	NORTH AMERICA
1988	9
1989	11
1990	18
1991	31
1992	38

SOURCE: Evan Mills, Lawrence
Berkeley Laboratory, Berkeley,
Calif., private communication,
February 3, 1993.

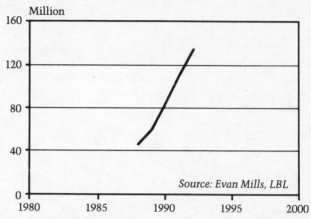

Figure 1: World Sales of Compact Fluorescent Bulbs, 1988–92

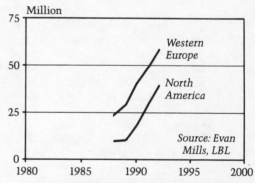

Figure 2: Sales of Compact Fluorescent Bulbs, North America and Western Europe, 1988–92

Atmospheric
Trends

CFC Production Falling

Lester R. Brown

In 1992, world production of chlorofluorocarbons (CFCs) declined more than 12 percent. (See Figures 1 and 2.) Falling for the fourth consecutive year, output is now 50 percent below the historical high reached in 1988.[1] This planned decline reflects the international community's commitment to protect life on earth from dangerous ultraviolet radiation by phasing out the family of chemicals that is depleting the stratospheric ozone layer.

When Sherwood Rowland and Mario Molina at the University of California hypothesized in 1974 that CFCs rising into the upper stratosphere could deplete ozone, many scientists were concerned.[2] When a team of British scientists reported in 1985 that they had found a decrease in ozone during the Antarctic spring, concern turned to alarm.[3]

Two years later, a U.N.-sponsored international conference in Montreal negotiated an agreement to cut CFC production in half over the next decade.[4] As new information indicated that the stratospheric ozone losses were not confined to the Antarctic, a second meeting was called in London in June 1990. Recognizing the urgency of the problem, the countries represented agreed to stop producing CFCs completely by the year 2000.[5] With results showing ever larger ozone losses, 87 countries met in Copenhagen in November 1992 and agreed to again advance the phaseout date, this time moving it to January 1, 1996.[6]

Substitutes for CFCs are being found for almost every major use. Hydrocarbons have replaced them as aerosol propellants and as blowing agents for some plastic foams. Those needing solvents for cleaning and other purposes are turning to aqueous and semiaqueous systems, to alcohol, and to other solvents.[7] In many countries, CFC recovering and recycling equipment is being installed to reclaim the chemical when refrigerators and air conditioners are serviced or scrapped.[8]

The trends in ozone depletion are reasonably well established. The size of the ozone hole over Antarctica during the spring has been large in each of the last four years. Year-round ozone losses have been observed at all latitudes outside the tropics.[9] A large body of scientific information supports the conclusion that the ozone losses are caused by emissions of human-made compounds containing chlorine and bromine.[10]

Data gathered by the Total Ozone Mapping Spectrometer aboard the Nimbus-7 satellite indicate that between 1979 and 1991, mid-latitude readings at 45 degrees south and 45 degrees north picked up a loss of ozone of 2–6 percent, with the actual loss depending on the time of the year and the region.[11] Less is known about the amount of ultraviolet radiation reaching the earth's surface, but, as expected, there appear to be heavy increases in Antarctica. Also of concern are recent data indicating that the ozone-layer depletion in the northern hemisphere occurs not only in the winter but also in spring and summer, a change that could affect crop production, since plants are most vulnerable in the early stages of growth.[12]

If countries comply completely with the Montreal Accord, as amended in London, stratospheric concentrations of ozone-depleting free chlorine (from CFCs) will peak around the year 2000 at 4.12 parts per billion by volume (ppbv). After this, chlorine concentrations are expected to slowly decline, reaching 3 ppbv in 2037 and 2 ppbv in 2066. At this level, which is the same as when the hole first appeared in the late seventies, it is believed that the ozone layer over Antarctica would recover.[13] Compliance with the Copenhagen agreements will accelerate the recovery.

At present, many countries are actually moving even faster than agreed to at the London conference, largely because of mounting scientific concern. Yet developing countries may have difficulty maintaining the schedule. To help them, the London conference agreed to create a Multilateral Fund to which some 35 countries pledged financial contributions to assist with the development of substitutes and the acquisition of recycling equipment. In 1991, $53 million was assessed (of which $39 million was paid by late 1992), and in 1992 the fund assessment increased to $73 million.[14] At the Copenhagen meeting, funding was increased to $113 million for 1993.[15]

ESTIMATED GLOBAL CFC PRODUCTION, 1950–92

YEAR	TOTAL[1]	USED AS PROPELLANT
		(thousand tons)
1950	42	—
1951	75	—
1952	52	—
1953	65	—
1954	71	—
1955	86	—
1956	103	—
1957	110	—
1958	105	—
1959	125	—
1960	150	121
1961	170	137
1962	210	171
1963	250	195
1964	290	228
1965	330	255
1966	390	296
1967	440	333
1968	510	379
1969	580	421
1970	640	467
1971	690	492
1972	790	546
1973	900	619
1974	970	670
1975	860	480
1976	920	485
1977	880	406
1978	880	366
1979	850	317
1980	880	310
1981	890	293
1982	870	284
1983	950	293
1984	1,050	304
1985	1,090	310
1986	1,130	316
1987	1,250	321
1988	1,260	275
1989	1,150	198
1990	820	137
1991 (prel)	720	93
1992 (prel)	630	80

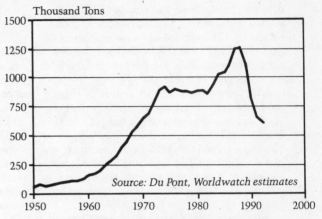

Figure 1: World Production of Chlorofluorocarbons, 1950–92

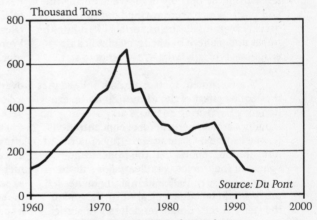

Figure 2: Production of CFCs for Use as Aerosol Propellants, 1960–92

[1]Includes all CFCs (CFC-11, CFC-12, CFC-113, CFC-114, and CFC-115).
SOURCE: Data for 1950–59 are Worldwatch Institute estimates based on data from Chemical Manufacturers Association; data for 1960–92 from E.I. Du Pont de Nemours, Wilmington, Del., private communication, March 5, 1993.

In 1992, the global average temperature dropped, falling from an average of 15.41 degrees Celsius in 1991 to 15.13 degrees.[1] (See Figure 1.) Although not as warm as some recent years, 1992 was still well above the average for the years 1951-80, the period used by meteorologists as a reference period.

After more than a decade of steadily rising temperatures that yielded a record high of 15.47 degrees Celsius in 1990, the June 1991 eruption of Mount Pinatubo in the Philippines may have given the world a brief respite from global warming.[2] The explosion injected vast amounts of sulfate aerosols into the upper atmosphere, which quickly spread around the globe.

Once there, these aerosols reflected a small amount of incoming sunlight back into space, thus exerting a cooling effect. In contrast to particles in the lower atmosphere, such as those from the burning of oil wells during the Gulf War, which were washed out rather quickly by rainfall, the materials lifted into the upper atmosphere by the force of volcanic eruptions typically take a few years to settle out.

U.S. government meteorologists believe that the cooling effect of the Mount Pinatubo eruption may be nearing an end. Larry Stowe, who monitors atmospheric aerosol concentrations for the National Oceanic and Atmospheric Administration, reports that the upper atmosphere in the tropics was cleared of sulfate aerosols by early 1993 and that the higher latitudes would be largely cleared by the end of the year.[3] If the climate modelers who anticipated the temperature fall caused by the volcanic eruption with such precision are correct, then the temperature rise under way since the early seventies could resume in the near future.

Although the precise effect on temperature of rising amounts of greenhouse gases is debatable, measurement of the rising concentrations of greenhouse gases in the atmosphere is extraordinarily precise. Official collection of data, which began in 1958, shows atmospheric concentrations of the principal greenhouse gas—carbon dioxide—rising every year since then, from 315.8 to 356.2 parts per million in 1992.[4] (See Figure 2.) Both this rise of 13 percent since 1959 and the anticipated continuing increase constitute one of the more ominous trends affecting the future habitability of the planet.

The projections of future temperature rise, assuming the continued burning of fossil fuels as projected, would lead to a rise in average global temperature in the late twenty-first century of 1.5–4.5 degrees—reaching between 16.5–19.5 degrees Celsius.[5]

World agriculture, which has evolved over the last 10,000 years during a period of remarkable climate stability, would be directly affected. Any major climate shift would be extraordinarily disruptive. During the summer of 1988, severe heat and drought in the United States dropped the U.S. grain harvest below domestic consumption for the first time in history.[6] Nonetheless, with grain reserves at a near-record level, the United States was able to satisfy the import needs of some 100 countries by exporting much of its vast reserves. Were such a disruption to occur in the mid-nineties, when reserves are comparatively low, world grain prices could easily double overnight, as they did between 1972 and 1973 following a massive shortfall in the Soviet harvest.[7]

The projected rise in global average temperature is expected to cause a rise in sea level of 18 centimeters (7 inches) by 2030 and 44 centimeters (17 inches) by 2070 due to both thermal expansion of the oceans and the melting of mountain glaciers.[8] Such a development offers a specter of vast displacements of people. Low-lying regions of the U.S. Mississippi delta, the lower Nile River valley, and many of the rice-growing river floodplains of Asia would be inundated. Losing that much cropland at a time when there will be far more people in the world would further intensify pressure on the land.

GLOBAL AVERAGE TEMPERATURE
AND ATMOSPHERIC CONCENTRATION
OF CARBON DIOXIDE, 1950–92

YEAR	TEMPERATURE (degrees Celsius)	CARBON DIOXIDE (parts per million)
1950	14.86	
1951	14.98	
1952	15.04	
1953	15.14	
1954	14.93	
1955	14.94	
1956	14.83	
1957	15.10	
1958	15.10	
1959	15.05	315.8
1960	14.98	316.8
1961	15.08	317.5
1962	15.02	318.3
1963	15.02	318.8
1964	14.74	—
1965	14.85	319.9
1966	14.91	321.2
1967	14.98	322.0
1968	14.88	322.8
1969	15.03	323.9
1970	15.04	325.3
1971	14.89	326.2
1972	14.93	327.3
1973	15.19	329.5
1974	14.93	330.1
1975	14.95	331.0
1976	14.78	332.0
1977	15.16	333.7
1978	15.09	335.3
1979	15.14	336.7
1980	15.28	338.5
1981	15.39	339.8
1982	15.07	341.0
1983	15.29	342.6
1984	15.11	344.3
1985	15.11	345.7
1986	15.16	347.0
1987	15.32	348.8
1988	15.35	351.4
1989	15.25	352.8
1990	15.47	354.0
1991	15.41	355.4
1992 (prel)	15.13	356.2

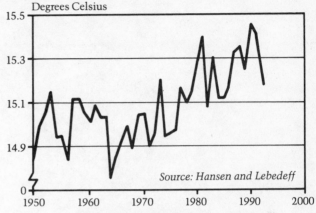

Figure 1: Global Average Temperature, 1950–92

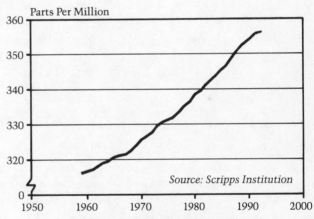

Figure 2: Atmospheric Concentrations of
Carbon Dioxide, 1959–92

SOURCES: Temperature data from J. Hansen and S.
Lebedeff, "Global Surface Air Temperatures:
Update Through 1987," Geophysical Research
Letters, Vol. 15, No. 4, 1988; Helene Wilson,
Columbia University and NASA Goddard Institute
for Space Studies, New York, private
communication, February 23, 1993; carbon dioxide
data from Charles O. Keeling (for 1959–90) and
Timothy Whorf (for 1991–92), Scripps Institute of
Oceanography, La Jolla, Calif., private
communications, February 26, 1993.

Note: The temperature series reported in Vital Signs
1992 was 3 degrees Celsius too low due to an error
made when converting from Fahrenheit.

Economic Trends

Global Economy Expands Slowly
Lester R. Brown

In 1992, the world economy, measured by gross world product (GWP), expanded by 1 percent, a modest increase over 1991, when there was virtually no growth.[1] (See Figure 1.) The expansion would be even less, or quite possibly negative, if national economic accounting systems subtracted the environmentally damaging effects of economic activity—destruction of the ozone layer, the medical costs of environmentally induced illness, the loss of topsoil, and so on—from the output totals.

This 1992 economic performance led to a second consecutive fall in per capita GWP, adding up to a 2.9 percent decline since 1990. (See Figure 2.) In dollar terms, average GWP per person for the world fell from $3,940 in 1990 to $3,827 in 1992.[2] With the International Monetary Fund projecting global growth in 1993 at scarcely 2 percent, it will take strong world economic performances in 1994 and 1995 merely to get per capita GWP back to the 1990 level by mid-decade.[3]

In large measure, the weak global performance was linked to simultaneous downturns in the world's three largest economies—the United States, Japan, and Germany.[4] Economic recovery in the United States is hampered by the vast federal deficit. The unexpectedly high cost of unification in Germany led to high interest rates, designed to check inflation. This in turn greatly reduced expansion in an otherwise robust economy. And Japan, experiencing a loss of investor confidence as its real estate bubble burst, is at best limping along.

Within the developing world, the Middle East and Asia, which contain half the world's people, had gains of roughly 10 and 7 percent, respectively. Africa, meanwhile, expanded at 2 percent, leading to yet another annual decline in the region's per capita economic output and extending the decline under way for more than a decade.[5]

The greatest economic disparities exist among the former centrally planned economies. In China, following economic reforms launched in 1978, the economy expanded by 12 percent in 1992, lifting income per person by nearly 11 percent.[6] In contrast, economic output declined an average of 19 percent in the 15 republics that make up the former Soviet Union, where economic reforms are quite recent.[7] This dramatic and unprecedented decline reflects far-reaching political and economic reforms designed to convert one centrally planned economy into 15 relatively independent market-driven ones.

Within Poland, the first East European country to launch economic reforms as the wave of democratization spread through the region, harsh early steps are now paying off. This reviving economy actually registered some growth in 1992 and is expected to achieve even more in 1993.[8]

The global downturn in the early nineties is the third major global recession since mid-century. The other two, in 1974–76 and 1980–81, were triggered by dramatic oil price hikes. The current problems are due in large part to economic mismanagement, as noted regarding the United States, Germany, and Japan, but there are new constraints emerging on global economic expansion, many of them little noticed by economists. These are physical constraints imposed by the earth's natural systems, including forests, grasslands, fisheries, and the hydrological cycle.

In China, the Indian subcontinent, and semiarid Africa, areas that contain nearly half of humanity, the demand for firewood and lumber exceeds forest regeneration by a wide margin.[9] Similarly, the production of beef and mutton in industrial and developing countries alike is pushing against grasslands' natural limits.[10] With fisheries, U.N. Food and Agriculture Organization marine biologists believe that the nearly 100 million tons being harvested annually represents the upper limit that can be sustained.[11] And in many countries, water scarcity is commonplace, constraining agricultural and, in some cases, industrial expansion.[12]

The effects of these environmental constraints on economic expansion are still modest at the global level, but they are growing. And they affect low-income agrarian economies disproportionately. Just as the rise in energy prices slowed global economic growth beginning in the mid-seventies, so environmental degradation and constraints are likely to slow it further during the nineties.

GROSS WORLD PRODUCT, 1950–92

YEAR	TOTAL (trill. 1987 dollars)	PER CAPITA (1987 dollars)
1950	3.8	1,487
1955	4.9	1,860
1960	6.1	2,236
1961	6.4	2,303
1962	6.7	2,366
1963	7.0	2,424
1964	7.5	2,548
1965	7.9	2,636
1966	8.3	2,732
1967	8.6	2,793
1968	9.1	2,903
1969	9.7	3,027
1970	10.1	3,083
1971	10.5	3,139
1972	11.0	3,221
1973	11.7	3,358
1974	11.8	3,319
1975	11.9	3,279
1976	12.5	3,375
1977	13.0	3,437
1978	13.5	3,497
1979	14.0	3,557
1980	14.1	3,514
1981	14.3	3,500
1982	14.4	3,463
1983	14.8	3,498
1984	15.4	3,578
1985	16.0	3,654
1986	16.4	3,681
1987	17.0	3,752
1988	17.8	3,862
1989	18.4	3,923
1990	18.8	3,940
1991	18.7	3,853
1992 (prel)	18.9	3,827

SOURCES: World Bank and International Monetary Fund; gross world product data for 1950 and 1955 from Herbert R. Block, *The Planetary Product in 1980: A Creative* Pause? (Washington, D.C.: U.S. Department of State, 1981); Center for International Research, U.S. Bureau of the Census, Washington, D.C., private communication, March 26, 1993; Worldwatch Institute.

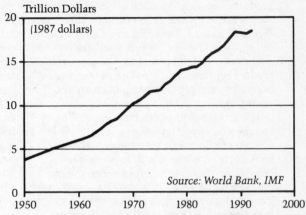

Figure 1: Gross World Product, 1950–92

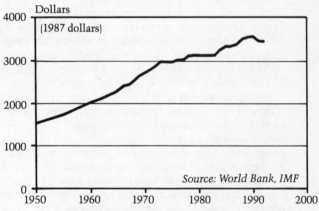

Figure 2: Gross World Product Per Person, 1950–92

Trade Continues Steep Rise   Hal Kane

In 1992, the value of internationally traded goods reached $3.58 trillion (in 1990 dollars), almost 20 percent of gross world product.[1] (See Figures 1 and 2.) From a figure of $308 billion in 1950, world trade has increased almost every year, and the percentage of gross world product represented by trade has increased even more steeply. The exceptions are the years following the two oil shocks.

The growth stems both from expanding commercial opportunities and from trade laws made more liberal by governments that believe in free trade as a path to economic growth. In 1947, for example, when the current system of trade laws was established, tariffs worldwide averaged almost 40 percent of the price of each product. Today, they average about 5 percent.[2] The European Community, the world's largest trading bloc, has eliminated tariffs completely within its borders.

Developing countries have increasingly embraced exports and open economies as the path to development, reversing some of the beliefs of the sixties and seventies, when many of them shut out foreign competition. And international organizations like the International Monetary Fund and World Bank have strongly encouraged open trade.

Private corporations, meanwhile, now often send products across national borders and have widely dispersed factories and offices. Global trade of products made by the world's 350 largest transnational corporations accounts for almost 40 percent of world merchandise trade.[3] Transnationals often rely on specialized production using lower-price labor from one region, cheap materials from another, markets in a third, and financing from a fourth.

The effects of growing trade have been mixed. In Europe, it is often credited with helping fuel dynamic economic growth since World War II. But since the mid-eighties, European economies have grown more slowly, and their finance ministers have looked to financial integration with a common currency, common social policies, and a federated European political system to strengthen and go beyond their trading bloc.

In some parts of the Third World, much of the revenues and economic development that trade was meant to generate have never materialized. Many of those countries have not found products that they can sell, at adequate prices, to other countries. Commodities like coffee, cocoa, and minerals have been oversupplied by the large number of exporters and, in some cases, subject to substitution from more easily available products, driving prices down.

Prices for nonfuel commodities were 30 percent lower in 1989 than in 1975 in real terms.[4] In 1990, the value of all exports from developing countries totalled $739 billion—scarcely 20 percent of the world total,[5] even though almost 80 percent of the world lives in these nations. Although industrial countries have signed preferential agreements with many developing countries, which make tariffs quite low, these have excluded some of the products that developing countries could compete the most strongly in, such as textiles, flowers, and food crops.[6]

Five countries in East Asia have broken out of that stagnation and grown explosively by emphasizing exports of such products as electronics, silverware, and clothes. But once those countries took over much of the market for such goods, they kept their market shares, and other countries have not had much success in following.[7]

For the environment, the effects of growing trade are mixed. On the one hand, competition from foreign firms through trade has stimulated some companies to improve manufacturing processes to make them use fewer resources and less energy. And it has spread important products in fields like medicine and environmental cleanup.

On the other hand, intensive production of crops has sometimes taken place in areas not well suited to them because production decisions were based on short-term economic gains and subsidies rather than the capacities of soil, water, and forests. Heavily polluting industries have sometimes migrated to the regions less able to control pollution with clean technologies and well-planned laws. And the transportation required to move goods has meant more use of fossil fuels, with associated pollution and extraction costs.[8]

WORLD EXPORTS, 1950–92

YEAR	EXPORTS (bill. 1990 dollars)
1950	308
1951	395
1952	370
1953	367
1954	383
1955	458
1956	498
1957	516
1958	512
1959	565
1960	620
1961	644
1962	691
1963	737
1964	808
1965	861
1966	927
1967	971
1968	1,093
1969	1,214
1970	1,326
1971	1,407
1972	1,533
1973	1,735
1974	1,853
1975	1,748
1976	1,948
1977	2,022
1978	2,132
1979	2,308
1980	2,328
1981	2,320
1982	2,223
1983	2,292
1984	2,510
1985	2,571
1986	2,577
1987	2,764
1988	3,004
1989	3,204
1990	3,331
1991 (prel)	3,417
1992 (prel)	3,554

SOURCE: Worldwatch calculations based on IMF data and deflators.

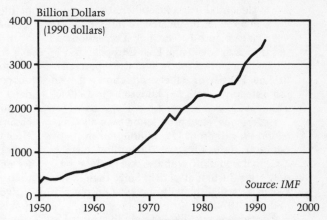

Figure 1: World Exports, 1950–92

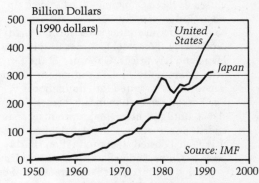

Figure 2: U.S. and Japanese Exports, 1951–92

Steel Production Falls Hal Kane

After peaking at 786 million tons in 1989, world steel production has fallen for three years in a row, dropping to 714 million tons in 1992.[1] (See Figure 1.) The global recession and reductions in Soviet and East European production accounted for most of the 9-percent decline. Per person, steel production fell even more steeply—from 151 kilograms in 1989 to 130 in 1992. (See Figure 2.)

Historically, steel production took off after World War II. From 112 million tons in 1946, output rose steadily, past 700 million tons in 1974, before falling with the rest of the economy after the first oil shock. Since then, it has grown only slightly, with the 1992 output close to that in 1974.[2]

Production is not likely to climb again anytime soon. The drops in the former Soviet Union and Eastern Europe that cut world production through 1992 may gradually be reversed as those economies start to pick up again. But as of early 1993, West European countries began ending subsidies that had propped up their steel factories despite low demand and low prices. One third of the European Community's total production—50 million tons—is targetted for elimination.[3] Further, all production in the former Yugoslavia, until recently a major producer, has ended.[4] Meanwhile, some developing countries have boosted steel production sharply, especially China, India, South Korea, and Iran.[5]

Making steel requires large amounts of energy. For the United States in 1988, 2,067 trillion Btus of energy were consumed producing steel from ore and scrap, and an additional 51 trillion Btus were used mining iron and other ores needed mainly to make steel.[6] That is almost as much energy as U.S. households consumed in electricity that year.[7] Much of the energy consumed by steelmaking comes from coal, and so is highly polluting.

Other countries have much less efficient factories and few or no regulations, so their pollution is far worse. The world's largest steel mill, the Magnitogorsk Metallurgical Complex in Russia, opened at the beginning of Stalin's first five-year plan, and now spews 800,000 tons of chemicals into the air every year. Half of the city's adults suffer from respiratory diseases.[8]

Plants like that are closing because of competition from more efficient firms, so pollution from steel production will tend to go down over time. Without a sweeping modernization at a cost of $10 billion, for example, the Magnitogorsk plant will shut soon because it cannot compete with other manufacturers.[9] Indeed, before its breakup, the Soviet Union produced 154 million tons in 1990 in such archaic plants, more than any other country.[10] Now that many of the plants are closing, world steel production may not regain its 1989 high for many years, if ever—nor its level of pollution.

Even among more-efficient mills, competition is adding to efficiency. While traditional steelmakers are struggling in many countries, including the United States, new firms that recycle scrap steel—and hence pollute much less—are thriving. Dubbed "minimills" for their small size and flexible manufacturing processes, these facilities use electric arc furnaces instead of older blast oxygen furnaces and can capitalize on massive existing stocks of steel in today's worn-out cars, outdated machines, and recyclable girders.[11]

In the industrial countries' "era of materials," which spanned two centuries, steel production was important to economic expansion; today, the level of materials use will no longer be such an important indicator of economic progress. The change has three explanations: a saturation of steel markets, substitution of other materials for steel, and new products that have a low materials content or use materials more efficiently.[12]

For developing countries, however, steel output may continue to grow for a long time. They will be stocking up on buildings, roads, and machines as their populations and economies grow. In 1990, developing countries produced 102 million tons of steel compared with industrial countries' 390 million tons, even though the former had three times as many people, and much of the developing-country production went to industrial nations as exports.[13] That inequality may shrink over time as production stagnates or shrinks in the North while it rises in the South.

WORLD STEEL PRODUCTION, 1959–92

YEAR	PRODUCTION (mill. tons)	PER CAPITA (kilograms per person)
1950	190	74
1951	211	81
1952	212	80
1953	235	88
1954	224	82
1955	270	97
1956	284	100
1957	293	101
1958	272	92
1959	307	102
1960	347	114
1961	346	112
1962	352	112
1963	378	118
1964	428	131
1965	450	135
1966	469	137
1967	493	142
1968	524	147
1969	571	157
1970	595	161
1971	582	154
1972	630	163
1973	696	177
1974	703	175
1975	644	157
1976	675	162
1977	675	160
1978	716	166
1979	747	171
1980	716	161
1981	707	156
1982	645	140
1983	664	141
1984	710	149
1985	719	148
1986	714	144
1987	736	146
1988	780	152
1989	786	151
1990	770	145
1991	736	137
1992 (prel)	714	130

SOURCE: International Iron and Steel Institute, *Steel Statistical Yearbook 1992* (Brussels: 1992).

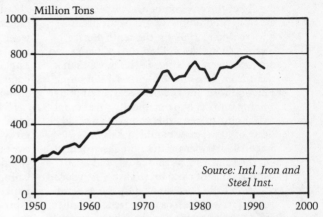

Figure 1: World Crude Steel Production, 1950-92

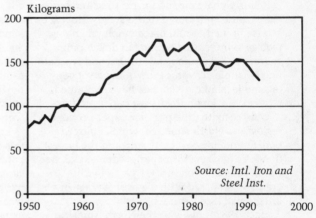

Figure 2: World Crude Steel Production Per Person, 1950–92

Paper Production Continues Growth   Ed Ayres

Despite a global recession and mounting concerns about the environmental impacts of wood pulp production, world paper production increased in 1992 for the tenth consecutive year. About 246 million tons of paper and paperboard were produced—up more than 2 percent from 1991.[1] (See Figure 1.) But while production rose, the industry staggered under a growing burden of overcapacity, oversupply, and declining prices—due in part to a rapid buildup of new paper plants in Asia.

Since 1950, paper production has grown at about the same rate as that of oil, and even faster than that of cars. Increases in newsprint production have been slowed by the general decline of newspapers, as hundreds of dailies either closed or merged in the face of competition from television and radio. For all other grades of paper, however, demand has boomed—expanding sixfold.[2]

Rising global demand for printing and office paper can be attributed to the steady growth of service industries and office employment, as well as to increasing literacy in developing countries. Revolutions in printing and typesetting technologies, plus growth in use of copying and facsimile machines, have facilitated rapid expansion in the use of paper products.

Until recently, the premier paper-producing region was North America, which enjoyed both abundant sources of pulp and the largest domestic markets for paper products. U.S. per capita consumption in 1991 was 314 kilograms—compared with a world average of 45 kilograms.[3] (See Figure 2.)

Since 1987, however, the North American share of world production has dropped from 50 percent to about 37 percent.[4] Much of the lost share was taken over by Asian producers. Although Japan—the second-largest producer of paper, despite a lack of forests—cut its output slightly in 1992, China increased by 10 percent and appeared likely to overtake Canada as the third largest producer in 1993.[5] Korea had the fastest growth of any country, with an increase of nearly 30 percent in 1992.[6]

The Indonesian and Malaysian pulp industries have also grown rapidly, and the increased use of tropical forests for commercial products (and the clearing of forest to grow pulp plantations) has heightened concerns about the impacts of the paper industry.[7] Making paper may use up as many as 4 billion trees per year.[8] With the world's annual net loss of forest now equal to an area larger than England, the paper and pulp industries have come under increasing pressure to find more sustainable sources.[9]

Help has come from three sources: wastepaper recycling, development of faster-growing varieties of trees (requiring less land over the long term), and increasing use of nonwood pulp. In Asian countries other than China and Japan, nearly 70 percent of used paper is recycled. In Europe, the recovery rate is above 50 percent, and the U.S. rate is about 34 percent—of which most is used for products like tissue and packaging.[10]

Asian producers have gained ground in this industry by developing more advanced methods in both waste-paper utilization and the use of such alternatives to trees as straw, bamboo, kenaf, jute, and bagasse (sugarcane waste). Since 1991, a Japanese company has begun to manufacture high-quality coated (glossy) magazine paper consisting of 80 percent recycled newspapers, and Chinese manufacturers are making 60 percent of their paper from nonwood sources.[11]

Environmental concerns have also been raised about the use of chlorine to bleach paper for printing. Evidence that this causes cancer and other forms of biological damage has generated strong pressures to develop alternatives. Europe has led in this area, rapidly expanding its capacity to produce "totally chlorine-free" paper.[12]

North American producers, slow to accept consumer demand for more recycled content and less chlorine bleaching, have been stung by their loss of market share and are now responding faster. Despite severe financial constraints during the recession, most major producers have invested heavily in processes and products that are more environmentally benign.[13]

WORLD PAPER AND PAPERBOARD
PRODUCTION, 1950–92

YEAR	PRODUCTION (mill. tons)	PER CAPITA (kilograms)
1950	46	18.0
1951	47	18.1
1952	46	17.5
1953	49	18.3
1954	52	19.1
1955	56	20.2
1956	60	21.2
1957	60	20.8
1958	61	20.7
1959	66	22.0
1960	69	22.7
1961	78	25.3
1962	81	25.8
1963	86	26.8
1964	92	28.1
1965	97	29.0
1966	104	30.5
1967	107	30.7
1968	114	32.1
1969	123	33.9
1970	128	34.6
1971	130	34.4
1972	139	36.0
1973	148	37.6
1974	151	37.6
1975	132	32.3
1976	148	35.6
1977	154	36.4
1978	160	37.2
1979	171	39.1
1980	170	38.2
1981	171	37.7
1982	167	36.2
1983	177	37.7
1984	190	39.8
1985	193	39.8
1986	202	40.9
1987	213	42.4
1988	225	44.0
1989	231	44.4
1990	239	45.1
1991	241	44.7
1992 (prel)	246	44.9

SOURCES: United Nations Statistical Office, *1988/89
Statistical Yearbook* (New York: 1992); *Pulp and
Paper International,* July 1991 and January 1993;
Worldwatch Institute.

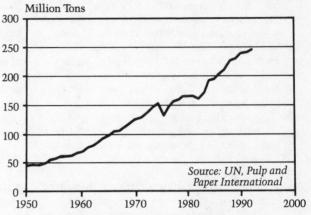

Million Tons

Source: UN, Pulp and
Paper International

Figure 1: World Paper Production, 1950–92

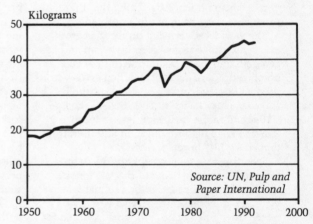

Kilograms

Source: UN, Pulp and
Paper International

Figure 2: World Paper Production Per Person, 1950–92

World Spending on Ads Skyrockets   Alan Thein Durning

Total global advertising expenditures multiplied nearly sevenfold from 1950 to 1990.[1] (See Figure 1.) They grew one third faster than the world economy and three times faster than world population.[2] In real terms, spending rose from $39 billion in 1950 to $256 billion in 1990—more than the gross national product of India or than all Third World governments spent on health and education.[3]

Measured in per capita terms, the growth of advertising is equally marked. In 1950, advertisers spent $15 for each person on the planet, while in 1970 they spent $27, and in 1990, $48.[4] (See Figure 2.)

Advertising spending is both a reflection of and a stimulus for the consumerism that is spreading among the world's people. High per capita resource use in the world's consumer societies is among the globe's principal ecological threats. Most advertising implicitly endorses consumerism, suggesting that there is a product to solve each of life's problems.[5]

The world's advertising budget has grown every year since recordkeeping began and has generally moved in tandem with total economic output, rising swiftly when gross world product boomed and more slowly when it stayed steady. Twice since 1950—in the late sixties and in the early eighties—advertising failed to keep up with inflation and therefore dipped slightly in real terms.[6]

Spending rose most steeply in the debt-financed economic boom of the late eighties, jumping by nearly $100 billion in just five years. That increase was spread equally between the United States (which accounted for three fourths of world advertising outlays at mid-century and still accounts for nearly half) and other countries.[7]

Americans are exposed to more advertising than anyone else on earth. U.S. marketers spent $468 per American in 1991, a figure that has grown from about $200 dollars per person in 1950 but is down from the 1990 peak of $500.[8] (See Figure 3.) The growth curve for U.S. advertising—rising and falling with economic output and soaring in the consumerist eighties—has shaped the growth curve for world advertising throughout the postwar period.

Among populous countries, Japan is second in the advertising league, dedicating more than $300 per citizen to sales pitches each year.[9] Western Europe is close behind: a typical person there is the target of more than $200 worth of ads a year.[10] The latest boom is under way in Eastern Europe, a region that John Lindquist of the Boston Consulting Group calls "an advertising executive's dream—people actually remember advertisements."[11]

Advertising is growing fast in developing countries as well, though it remains small-scale by western standards. Expenditures in China are less than 50¢ per person.[12] South Korea's advertising industry grew 35–40 percent annually in the late eighties, and yearly ad billings in India jumped fivefold in the eighties, surpassing $1 per person for the first time.[13] In Latin American countries such as Mexico and Brazil, ad outlays are about $25 per person.[14]

The premier medium for advertisers is commercial television, which has been gaining viewers around the world. During the eighties, governments deregulated or privatized television programming in most of Western Europe—allowing advertising on a scale previously witnessed only in the United States. In India, declares Gurcharan Das, chairman of Procter & Gamble India, "an advertiser can reach 200 million people every night" through television.[15] All told, perhaps half the world's people have ready access to commercial television broadcasts.[16]

The trajectory of spending on advertising, as both an indicator of consumerism and a tool of its advance, is an ominous portent for the global environment.

WORLD ADVERTISING EXPENDITURES, 1950–90

YEAR	TOTAL (bill. 1989 dollars)	PER CAPITA (1989 dollars)
1950	39	15
1960	74	28
1968	104	29
1970	99	27
1972	108	28
1974	115	29
1976	119	29
1977	133	31
1979	157	36
1980	164	37
1981	159	35
1982	157	34
1983	163	35
1985	164	34
1986	199	40
1987	222	44
1988	237	46
1989	247	47
1990	256	48

SOURCE: 1950 and 1960 from Robert J. Coen, *International Herald Tribune,* October 10, 1984, cited in Frederick Clairmonte and John Cavanagh, *Merchants of Drink* (Penang, Malaysia: Third World Network, 1988); more recent years from Tracy Poltie, International Advertising Association, New York, private communications, August 20, 1990, and January 15, 1992.

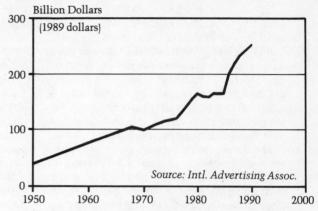

Figure 1: World Advertising Expenditures, 1950–90

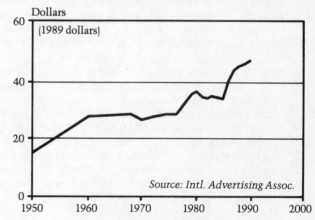

Figure 2: World Advertising Expenditures Per Person, 1950–90

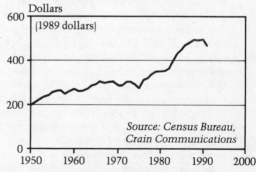

Figure 3: U.S. Advertising Expenditures Per Person, 1950–91

Third World Debt Rising Slowly

Hal Kane

The 1992 Third World external debt of $1.428 trillion was up slightly from $1.361 trillion the preceding year.[1] (See Figure 1.) While the rapid growth in debt of the eighties has been halted, slower growth remains.[2] And existing debt continues to discourage development by drawing away funds that could otherwise be put to productive use, and by forcing many developing countries to adopt economic policies aimed at managing debt rather than at fostering balanced, long-term development.

The classic recipe for development has been for countries to borrow money to invest in industry, education, and economic development. Governments intend to pay the debt back later from income earned by their investments, assuming that their economies will have become healthier and more able to pay. But in many countries, mismanagement and misguided investments have led to projects that failed to foster sound development or generate as much revenue as hoped. Those countries are now trying to meet debt payments without the benefit of adequate income from successful investments or growing economies.

Still suffering from many misplaced investment priorities and now also struggling to meet payments to creditors, they often are unable to direct their spending toward long-term improvements in their countries, and their development is stifled. Putting $10 billion a year into energy efficiency in the Third World, for example, would generate $1.75 trillion in saved costs on new sources of energy over 35 years, according to one study, while reducing pollution—but this investment is not being made.[3] And World Bank research shows that investments in women's literacy would pay themselves back in financial terms at 20 percent per year while lowering infant mortality and improving equity—but countries also are not making these investments.[4] The same is true for many similar promising opportunities.

In an effort to deal with indebtedness and to promote their version of development, the International Monetary Fund and the World Bank press debtor governments to accept structural adjustment programs. These include such things as devaluing currencies to encourage exports and discourage imports. The pro-

grams have cut subsidies and government spending on social programs to save money and weed out corruption, have kept wages low to discourage spending and inflation, and have reduced quotas and tariffs that inhibited international trade.[5]

Although these programs make some of the most wide-reaching and fundamental changes ever implemented by international institutions, analyses of their impacts have rarely included environmental effects, since these are outside traditional economic models. In 1992, however, some of the first comprehensive studies of these effects were published.[6]

In research on the Philippines, Robert Repetto and Wilfrido Cruz found several severe effects from one such program that received little or no attention from the economists who planned it. Because of the program's austerity, real wages fell more than 20 percent during two years of the program, leaving 58 percent of the population below the poverty line. One result was sharply accelerated migration by impoverished people into upland watersheds and coastal regions, intensifying deforestation and erosion and the overexploitation of coastal fisheries and mangroves. The planners knew that the adjustment programs put a particularly large burden on the poor, but they did not consider the environmental repercussions of that poverty, nor that environmental damage itself becomes a constraint on economic development.[7]

Although some of the goals of structural adjustment programs are admirable, they have not been balanced by corresponding programs to lessen the social and environmental burdens. As a result, they have not contributed to, and sometimes have hindered, efforts to spread education, health care, environmental protection, and other bases of development and long-term economic progress.

Meanwhile, investment of money in developing countries is only now regaining the levels of the early eighties. In the mid and late eighties, however, more money was paid by the developing countries to cover their loans than they received in additional funds. (See Figure 2.)

EXTERNAL DEBT OF ALL
DEVELOPING COUNTRIES, 1980–92

YEAR	DEBT (bill. dollars)
1980	639
1981	751
1982	846
1983	912
1984	943
1985	1,046
1986	1,147
1987	1,290
1988	1,282
1989	1,306
1990	1,355
1991	1,361
1992 (prel)	1,428

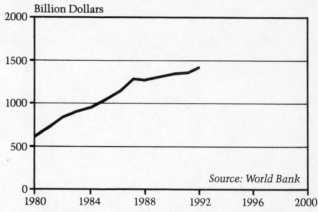

Figure 1. External Debt of Developing Countries, 1980–92

TOTAL NET TRANSFERS OF CAPITAL
FROM INDUSTRIAL TO DEVELOPING
COUNTRIES, 1980–92

YEAR	NET TRANSFER (bill. dollars)
1980	37
1981	46
1982	29
1983	14
1984	− 1
1985	− 3
1986	− 7
1987	− 7
1988	− 5
1989	3
1990	23
1991	29
1992	50

SOURCE: World Bank, *World Debt Tables 1991–92*
(Washington, D.C.: 1992); International Monetary
Fund, *World Economic Outlook,* January 1993;
World Bank, Washington, D.C., private
communication, April 27, 1993.

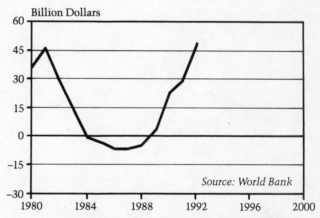

Figure 2: Net Movement of Public and Private Capital
From Industrial to Developing Countries, 1980–92

Transportation
Trends

Bicycle Production Resumes Climb   Ed Ayres

More than 100 million bicycles were produced in 1992—surpassing the previous year's production by more than 5 million.[1] (See Figure 1.) Despite a global recession, this reestablished a high growth trend of the past three decades that had been temporarily stalled by excess inventory in China.

The bicycle also continued to widen its lead over the automobile as the world's leading vehicle for personal transportation, extending a trend that began 23 years ago. In 1969, bicycles and cars were produced in almost equal numbers worldwide—25 million bicycles and 23 million cars.[2] But car production had been gaining fast as developing countries built roads and as incomes rose. It appeared likely that cars would overtake bikes as the most widely used vehicle in the seventies.

In 1970, however, global bicycle production surged, commencing a trend that has shown no signs of abating. While automobile production since then has increased by only half, bicycle production has quadrupled. In 1992, nearly three times as many bicycles as cars came off assembly lines.[3]

The production surge coincided with the first Earth Day, and with the emergence of the environmental and fitness movements in industrial countries. Many people found bikes to be a more environmentally friendly means of travel and a more active, healthful form of recreation.

In most countries, however, bicycles were purchased as primary transportation vehicles. Throughout the seventies, they were used increasingly for commuting in China and India, for hauling produce from fields to villages in Kenya and Indonesia, and for delivering mail in Tanzania.[4] Their primary advantages were their mobility and price; whereas fewer than 10 percent of the world's people could afford cars, about 80 percent could afford bikes.[5]

In the eighties, these benefits became clearer as the problems associated with cars—air pollution, high energy consumption, congestion, and disruption of urban space—became increasingly burdensome. Bicycles produce no pollution, require no energy other than the calories expended by the rider, do not encounter (or create) as much congestion, and are more compatible than cars are with what most people do in cities—whether it is work, study, recreation, or sleep.

As the world became more urbanized, the relative mobility of bikes continued to increase. In U.S. cities, bicycles are the preferred vehicle for small-package couriers. They are used by more than 100 police forces for patrolling city parks, drug-dealing neighborhoods, and other areas where cars are either too clumsy or too conspicuous.[6]

Bicycles are used most in China, where there are 250 bikes for every car.[7] (See Figure 2.) There are also 12 bikes for every refrigerator there and two bikes for every television—indications of their utilitarian importance in a country that can afford neither the capital cost nor the land required for an extensive automotive infrastructure.[8] In the agriculture-rich river valleys where many Chinese live, building an extensive road system for cars would severely diminish the country's food-producing capacity.

China is also the largest producer of bicycles; 36 million bikes were manufactured there in 1992, compared with 35 million cars produced in the whole world.[9] Other major bicycle producers were Japan, India, Taiwan, and the United States—each making just under 8 million. Next came Germany (5 million), followed by Brazil and Indonesia, with 2 million each.[10]

Although China has by far the largest bicycle fleet, the growth in bicycle production is not just a Third World phenomenon. The United States and China may have the world's highest and lowest per capita car ownership, but they have almost identical per capita bicycle ownership: 1 per 3 people.[11] Even with its high car ownership, the United States has about 4 million bicycle commuters.[12]

WORLD BICYCLE PRODUCTION, 1960–92

YEAR	PRODUCTION (million)
1950	11
1951	12
1952	12
1953	13
1954	14
1955	15
1956	16
1957	17
1958	18
1959	19
1960	20
1961	20
1962	20
1963	20
1964	21
1965	21
1966	22
1967	23
1968	24
1969	25
1970	36
1971	39
1972	46
1973	52
1974	52
1975	43
1976	47
1977	49
1978	51
1979	54
1980	62
1981	65
1982	69
1983	74
1984	76
1985	79
1986	84
1987	98
1988	105
1989	95
1990	95
1991	95
1992 (prel)	100

SOURCES: United Nations, *The Growth of World Industry 1969 Edition*, Vol. II (New York: 1971); United Nations, *Yearbooks of Industrial Statistics 1979 and 1989 Editions*, Vol. II (New York: 1981 and 1991); *Interbike Directory 1993* (Costa Mesa, Calif.: Primedia, Inc., 1993).

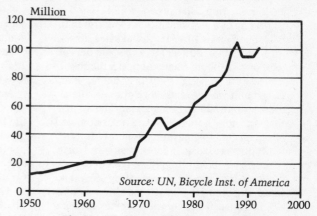

Figure 1: World Bicycle Production 1950–92

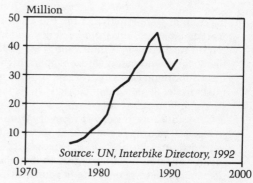

Figure 2: Bicycle Production in China, 1976–92

Auto Production Flat   Ed Ayres

World automobile production remained flat in 1992, reflecting widespread trouble—and the beginning of a global shakeout—in the industry.[1] (See Figure 1.) With global sales increasing by less than 200,000 from 1991's depressed total of 35 million, financial performances continued to sag among major producers.[2] Plants closed and work forces were cut heavily in most auto-producing countries.[3] The contraction was not solely due to the recession, and was expected to continue: General Motors (GM) plans to close 21 more plants in North America by the mid-nineties, Nissan expects to cut its work force by 8 percent by 1994, and Isuzu will stop producing cars altogether.[4]

One cause of the contraction was manufacturers' heavy—and optimistic—investments in new capacity during the eighties, which sales in the past three years have not been strong enough to pay for. Demand has been further depressed by low consumer confidence resulting from high unemployment in the leading market countries, and from currency and interest rate fluctuations in Europe. That has left many plants and manufacturers operating far below optimum capacity. Nissan, for example, ran at under 80 percent of capacity in its Japanese plants in 1992.[5]

Car sales showed signs of recovery from the severe 1991 slump in the United States, but were erratic in Europe and fell sharply in Japan.[6] The only significant growth in global demand came from developing countries such as South Korea, where both sales and production increased by about 15 percent in 1992.[7] But these nations constitute a small share of the world market. High per capita car ownership and slow population growth in the major markets left little room for further sales growth there during the past decade.

Obscured by the headlines about plant closings and layoffs are indications of major changes afoot—and a recognition that the automobile industry may be headed for significant reform.[8] The shakeups have brought changes on two levels: in the economics of manufacturing and in the role of the auto in a rapidly changing world.

Economically, the auto industry was described by analysts in 1992 as being in a crisis of unprecedented severity.[9] But this was not a sudden development; it had been unfolding over an extended period of flat growth in demand. The number of people per car has changed little in the past decade. (See Figure 2.) Production has remained essentially static for four years.

As a result, manufacturers have reassessed their operations, and—following the lead of the Japanese, who expanded with envied speed in the eighties—adopted new concepts of manufacturing. Thus even while traditional or obsolete plants close, new ones open with far more efficient processes and better quality. In 1992, GM's Opel subsidiary started a new plant in eastern Germany using "lean production" methods requiring just two thirds as many workers as a traditional plant with equivalent production capacity.[10]

Lean production has become the new byword of manufacturers. The concept combines just-in-time component deliveries, zero-defect strategies, and other changes from traditional methods. Nissan's newly opened British plant cut inventory for its European parts to 1.6 days, for example, compared with an industry average of 20 days.[11] By closing the "quality" gap, U.S. manufacturers began to regain some market share they had lost to the Japanese; over the past several years they reduced defects from about 7 per car to 1.5, while Japan went from 2 defects to 1.3.[12]

Even as manufacturers hustle to reduce production costs, however, the overall costs of cars are being redefined. "External" costs of congestion and air pollution, in particular, are creating pressures to change not only the manufacturing processes but also the nature of the car.[13] California, for instance, is compelling development of both new fuels and new engines, particularly electric vehicles.

Pressures are also growing to restrict auto use altogether—by reducing the need for transport or increasing the use of alternative modes. Japanese city-dwellers cannot own cars unless they can show proof of off-street parking.[14] U.S. and European cities are developing more park-and-ride public transit. As pressures grow to internalize external costs, they may further constrain growth.

WORLD AUTOMOBILE PRODUCTION, 1950–92

YEAR	PRODUCTION (million)
1950	8
1951	7
1952	6
1953	8
1954	8
1955	11
1956	9
1957	10
1958	9
1959	11
1960	13
1961	11
1962	14
1963	16
1964	17
1965	19
1966	19
1967	19
1968	22
1969	23
1970	22
1971	26
1972	28
1973	30
1974	26
1975	25
1976	29
1977	30
1978	31
1979	31
1980	29
1981	28
1982	27
1983	30
1984	30
1985	32
1986	33
1987	33
1988	34
1989	36
1990	36
1991	35
1992 (prel)	35

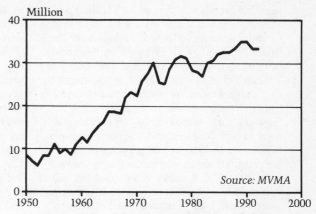

Figure 1: World Automobile Production, 1950–92

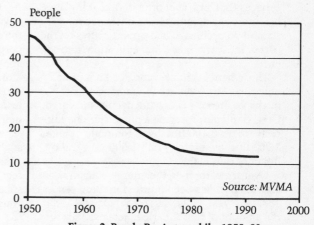

Figure 2: People Per Automobile, 1950–92

SOURCES: Motor Vehicle Manufacturers Association, *World Motor Vehicle Data,* 1991 ed. (Detroit, Mich.: 1991); 1992 estimate from American Automobile Manufacturers Association, Japan Automobile Manufacturers Association, and *Financial Times.*

Air Travel Growth Resumes
Hal Kane

World air travel increased 7 percent in 1992, reaching an all-time high of 1.97 trillion passenger-kilometers. (See Figure 1.) The rise represented a recovery from 1991, when for the first time travel by air dropped, by 3 percent, because of the Gulf War and global recession. Air cargo rose as well in 1992, up 5 percent to 61.2 million ton-kilometers carried.[1] (See Figure 2.)

After World War II, global air travel grew almost seventyfold—from 28 billion passenger-kilometers in 1950 to 1.89 trillion in 1990. For freight, the growth was similar, increasing from 800,000 ton-kilometers carried in 1950 to 58.8 million in 1990.[2] Growth in air transport was so strong that it overrode the economic downturns that followed the oil shocks of 1973 and 1979, probably because of quickly growing interdependence among regions and countries.[3] That strong growth reflected the many services that air travel provided, making possible improved communications, faster responses to problems, and opportunities on the part of industry, medicine, education, and science.

Those benefits have come at a high price, however. Airplanes are the most energy-intensive means of carrying people and cargo. On U.S. planes, carrying a passenger one kilometer takes 3,100 Btu; by automobile, it takes 2,200 Btu; by intercity rail, 1,500 Btu; and by intercity bus, 600.[4]

Over time, though, the energy efficiency of air transport has been improving. Between 1973, the year of the first oil shock, and 1984, the amount of fuel American jets used to carry each passenger one kilometer decreased by 70 percent, partly from the use of wider-body jets with more passengers on each flight and from more-efficient turbines.[5] Boeing's newest airplane, the 777, has a wider body and wingspan than any other plane and two engines instead of three or four. When it becomes available in 1995, it will require less energy to do the same work.[6]

Despite the improvements in efficiency, however, jet fuel use has climbed steadily because the total distance flown has gone up. For the world as a whole, only 472,000 tons of jet fuel were produced in 1950; by 1970, the figure reached 81 million tons and by 1990, 156 million tons.[7] That amounted to more than 10 percent of the world's consumption of transportation fuel.[8]

Americans lead the world in airplane fuel consumption, which increased from 187 kilograms of jet fuel per person in 1970 to 258 kilograms in 1990. Canada follows, with its consumption growing from 75 kilograms per person in 1970 to 123 in 1990. No other country of major size comes even close. Australia now uses 75 kilograms per person; the United Kingdom, 55; France, 24; Japan, 23; Germany, 19; and Bangladesh, just 1.[9]

Along with that consumption has come pollution. In 1990, the burning of jet fuel produced about 550 million tons of carbon dioxide, 220 million tons of water, 3.5 million tons of nitrogen oxides, and 180,000 tons of sulfur dioxide, says the International Energy Agency.[10]

What matters most about this pollution is the altitude at which it is released. At least 60 percent enters the air more than 9 kilometers above sea level, and as a result will stay in the atmosphere some 100 times longer than if it were released at ground level because it has fewer other molecules to react with. Furthermore, the concentrations of those gases—especially nitrogen oxides—is ordinarily low at such heights, so the additions cause extensive change and contribute to the greenhouse effect. And they can lead to increases of tropospheric ozone, which also adds to greenhouse warming.[11]

At lower heights, nitrogen oxides undergo different reactions, and they play a part in chemical processes that break down ozone molecules, possibly contributing to stratospheric ozone depletion.[12] Even the water released by air traffic, which would be harmless near the ground, causes disruption at high altitudes. It freezes in the cold upper sky, and the ice crystals allow sunlight through but then trap the energy radiating outward from the earth, thereby adding to global warming.[13]

WORLD AIR TRANSPORT, 1950–92

YEAR	PEOPLE (bill. passenger-kilometers)	FREIGHT (mill. ton-kilometers)
1950	28	0.8
1951	35	0.9
1952	40	1.0
1953	46	1.1
1954	52	1.1
1955	61	1.3
1956	71	1.5
1957	81	1.7
1958	85	1.7
1959	95	1.9
1960	115	2.2
1961	128	2.4
1962	136	2.9
1963	150	3.2
1964	171	4.0
1965	200	4.8
1966	230	5.6
1967	297	6.6
1968	308	7.9
1969	351	9.8
1970	460	12.0
1971	494	13.2
1972	560	15.0
1973	618	17.5
1974	656	19.0
1975	697	19.4
1976	762	21.4
1977	818	23.6
1978	934	26.4
1979	1,060	28.0
1980	1,089	29.3
1981	1,119	30.9
1982	1,142	31.5
1983	1,190	35.1
1984	1,278	39.6
1985	1,367	39.8
1986	1,452	43.2
1987	1,589	48.3
1988	1,709	53.6
1989	1,780	57.2
1990	1,894	58.8
1991	1,842	58.5
1992 (prel)	1,967	61.2

SOURCE: International Civil Aviation Organization, Montreal.

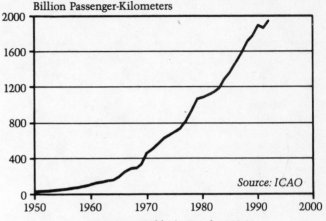

Billion Passenger-Kilometers

Source: ICAO

Figure 1: World Air Travel, 1950-91

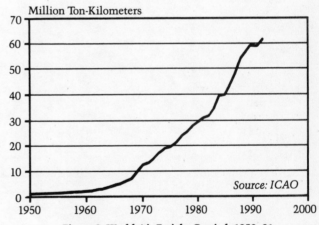

Million Ton-Kilometers

Source: ICAO

Figure 2: World Air Freight Carried, 1950–91

Social
Trends

Population Growth Sets Another Record   Linda Starke

The unrelenting arithmetic of population growth is once again receiving the attention of environmental groups, newspaper columnists, and government bureaucrats as the September 1994 U.N. World Population Conference in Cairo draws near. Last year, some 91 million people were added to the world's population, bringing the total number to 5.5 billion.[1] (See Figures 1 and 2.) So every month in 1992 we added nearly the equivalent of the population of New York City or Bolivia to the world.[2]

Africa, where per capita incomes are now lower than they were at the start of the eighties, continues to be the fastest growing continent.[3] Overall, the number of Africans is increasing 2.9 percent a year. The continent is currently home to 12 percent of the world's people; by 2025, when its numbers will have more than doubled, Africa is expected to account for 19 percent of world population.[4]

Latin America has the next most rapid growth rate, at 1.9 percent a year. Annual rates of natural increase there range from less than 1 percent in Barbados and Uruguay to above 3 in Guatemala and Honduras. Brazil is growing 1.5 percent a year, which will translate into an additional 2.3 million Brazilians in 1993.[5]

During the last few years, more accurate censuses have provided several surprises in some countries. One of the largest revisions concerned Nigeria. The government released census data in 1992 indicating a total population of 88.5 million, some 30 million fewer than had been thought.[6] This does not mean that population growth stopped in Nigeria—just that a better estimate of the number of people living there is available. It is still the most populous nation in Africa by far, and is growing at a rate that will lead to a doubling in 23 years if it is unchanged.[7]

Mexico released new census results in late 1991, with the total number of Mexicans tallied at some 7 million lower than had been expected.[8] Mexico City, often thought of as the largest city in the world, has slipped to number four in the ranking of the world's urban areas by population—behind Tokyo, São Paulo, and New York.[9] Again, this does not mean that population growth slowed dramatically in

Mexico, just that the government has a more accurate count of the residents. With nearly 4 in every 10 Mexicans under the age of 15, the nation has a huge built-in momentum for future population growth.[1]

The breakup of the Soviet Union has also shifted the demographic order. In 1990, the Soviet Union was the third most populous country in the world.[11] Now Russia, the largest republic, is in sixth place in the world ranking—behind China and India as well as the United States, Indonesia, and Brazil.[12] If current growth rates remain unchanged, Pakistan will soon push Russia even further down the list.

Statistics that once covered the entire Soviet Union have been broken down to show differing patterns of fertility, mortality, and urbanization in various ethnic subgroups. Women in the Soviet Union, for example, had on average 2.3 children.[13] In the new republics, the figure ranges from 5.2 in Tajikistan to 1.8 or lower in Belarus, Russia, and Ukraine.[14] Data such as these reinforce the importance of tailoring family planning and maternal health campaigns to the needs of particular groups.

The revision of national population totals and the refinement of data within nations have given us a better understanding of where the world stands in terms of current numbers. They have not, however, affected the daunting forecasts of continuing population increase. All our efforts to slow environmental degradation are made more difficult by the pressure of this growing population combined with the pressure of overconsumption of resources by the richest one fifth of humanity.[15]

During the seventies, the rate of increase in human numbers—though still considerable—was falling. If the decline had continued along the same path, world population would have reached zero growth at 6.7 billion in 2030. But the slowdown in the growth rate stalled in the eighties. The figure of 6.7 billion is now likely to be reached in 2005.[16] And by 2030, if the annual growth rate remains at the current level of 1.7 percent, world population could reach 10.7 billion—4 billion more people than would have been here had the trend of the seventies continued.[17]

WORLD POPULATION, TOTAL AND ANNUAL ADDITION, 1950–92

YEAR	POPULATION (billion)	ANNUAL ADDITION (million)
1950	2.554	37
1951	2.591	42
1952	2.633	45
1953	2.678	48
1954	2.726	51
1955	2.777	53
1956	2.830	56
1957	2.886	56
1958	2.942	52
1959	2.994	42
1960	3.036	41
1961	3.077	56
1962	3.133	70
1963	3.203	71
1964	3.274	69
1965	3.343	70
1966	3.413	69
1967	3.482	71
1968	3.553	74
1969	3.627	75
1970	3.702	78
1971	3.780	77
1972	3.857	77
1973	3.934	76
1974	4.010	74
1975	4.084	73
1976	4.157	73
1977	4.230	73
1978	4.302	76
1979	4.378	77
1980	4.454	76
1981	4.531	80
1982	4.611	81
1983	4.692	80
1984	4.771	81
1985	4.852	85
1986	4.938	87
1987	5.025	88
1988	5.113	88
1989	5.201	90
1990	5.291	87
1991	5.378	91
1992 (prel)	5.469	91

SOURCE: Center for International Research, U.S. Bureau of the Census, Washington, D.C., private communication, May 11, 1993, as revised.

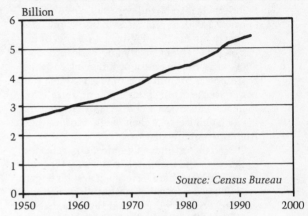

Figure 1: World Population, 1950–92

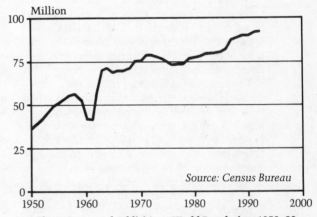

Figure 2: Annual Addition to World Population, 1950–92

Child Mortality Continues to Fall Hal Kane

The number of children in the world dying before their fifth birthday has fallen to 94 out of every 1,000, an impressive drop from 240 in the early fifties.[1] (See Figure 1.) The decline has been relatively steady and widespread. One of the world's most optimistic trends, it represents a combination of progress in a number of areas—from spreading immunizations to health education and others. Nevertheless, 250,000 children die each week, most of them from preventable diseases.[2]

U.N. data for under five mortality rates are projections and estimates, especially for the many regions where exact data are never gathered. They are based on assumptions about growing economies and food supplies that are not proving true in some areas. Future surveys may show deterioration in some regions, slowing or reversing today's optimistic trend. In most of Africa, for example, declining per capita incomes and reduced growth in grain production are signals that child mortality may be on the rise. Indeed, the fact that data are not available for many regions is itself an indicator of the barriers to improvement, and covers up some negative regional trends.

The first year of life is by far the most hazardous. Up until one year of age, infants are intensely dependent on mothers, so maternal health is a major determinant of their survival. Mothers who are well nourished and who breast-feed pass that nutrition and immunological protection on to babies, who then are much more able to fight disease.

Between the first and fifth years of life, children venture increasingly into their surroundings and become more affected by the outside environment. Food not coming from their mothers becomes important, and environmental conditions like urban sanitation and communicable diseases matter more than in the first year. Malnutrition is often behind the spread of disease, as it weakens children's immune systems. It is estimated to contribute to as many as 40 percent of all child deaths.[3]

The unequal distribution of incomes and wealth both among and within countries provides the backdrop for high infant and child death rates. Some 98 percent of all child deaths occur in the Third World, where inadequate incomes cause malnutrition and undermine access to clean water, sanitation, and adequate housing.[4] For developing countries as a whole, mortality rates of children under five are more than seven times those in the industrial world.[5] (See Figures 2 and 3.)

Some of the best progress has come from spreading immunizations. Smallpox has been eradicated, and many other diseases slowed effectively. The major diseases that kill the most children are well known and often can be attacked at low cost. Immunizations for diphtheria, whooping cough, measles, polio, tuberculosis, and tetanus reached only about 10 percent of children worldwide in the late seventies, but are reaching 80 percent today. About 3 million child deaths are now prevented each year by immunization.[6]

Still, spreading immunization even further holds some of the greatest potential for reducing deaths. Some 2 million children die every year for lack of access to available vaccines; another 5–6 million die from potentially preventable ailments such as malaria, respiratory infections, meningitis, and certain diarrheal diseases.[7]

Oral rehydration therapy (ORT) to treat diarrheal diseases also holds great potential, because dehydration is the largest single killer of children.[8] UNICEF points out that simple education and basic ORT supplies of salt and sugar packets saved more than 1 million children in 1990—and could save 2.5 million more—without requiring doctors or any major expenses. Vitamin A supplements and nutrition programs, breast-feeding promotion, birth spacing, and malaria preventions and cures also can lower mortality rates of children impressively.[9]

Educating mothers is especially important to reducing child mortality. The mortality rates of children of women with seven or more years of schooling, for example, are half as high as those of women with no formal education. Educated women are more likely to have enough status and power in their families to get prenatal care, delivery care, childhood immunizations, better diets for their children, and better housing.[10]

MORTALITY OF CHILDREN UNDER FIVE YEARS OLD, 1950–PRESENT

YEAR	WORLD (deaths per thousand children)
1950–55	240
1955–60	215
1960–65	182
1965–70	161
1970–75	144
1975–80	131
1980–85	118
1985–90	105
1990–95	94

YEAR	INDUSTRIAL COUNTRIES
1950–55	73
1955–60	51
1960–65	39
1965–70	32
1970–75	26
1975–80	24
1980–85	19
1985–90	17
1990–95	14

YEAR	DEVELOPING COUNTRIES
1950–55	281
1955–60	255
1960–65	213
1965–70	184
1970–75	164
1975–80	149
1980–85	134
1985–90	119
1990–95	106

SOURCE: United Nations, Department of International Economic and Social Affairs, *Mortality of Children Under Age 5: World Estimates and Projections, 1950–2025* (New York: 1988).

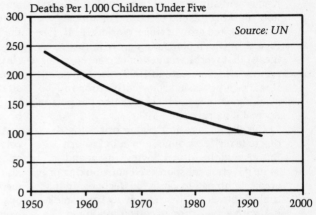

Figure 1: World Child Mortality, 1950–55 to 1990–95

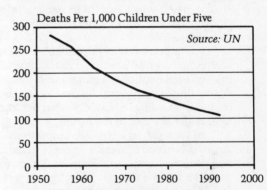

Figure 2: Child Mortality in Developing Countries, 1950–55 to 1990–95

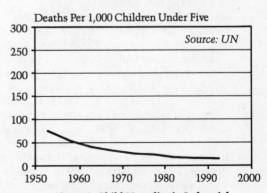

Figure 3: Child Mortality in Industrial Countries, 1950–55 to 1990–95

Cigarette Smoking Drops Again   Hal Kane

The number of cigarettes produced in 1992 held essentially constant from 1991 at 5.39 trillion, marking the end of a trend of almost uninterrupted growth since World War II. (See Figure 1.) Given population growth, this means that world production of cigarettes per person fell 1.7 percent in 1992. (See Figure 2.) It marked the second consecutive drop in smoking, with cigarette production per person down 4.4 percent since 1990.[1]

The global recession, higher prices (partly due to taxes), economic reform in Eastern Europe and the former Soviet Union, and some government-sponsored antismoking programs combined to cause the declines. Industrial countries led the trend away from smoking, with a 1992 drop in consumption per person over the age of 18 of 3 percent in the United States, which has cut its per capita smoking rate in half since the record in 1963. (See Figure 3.)[2]

As the largest cause of preventable disease and premature death in the industrial world, tobacco consumption is a major indicator of the health of populations; for developing countries, it is a leading indicator of what are likely to be major diseases in the future.

Until recently, cigarette consumption was largely a function of wealth—people in industrial countries tend to smoke more. Japan, for example, has one of the world's highest rates, at 2,533 cigarettes per person every year. The United States and Germany likewise have some of the highest rates per person, at 2,140 and 2,004 cigarettes respectively, despite strong antismoking education campaigns.[3] Recently, though, smoking has declined in some of the wealthiest nations.

Countries whose economies have grown quickly have watched their smoking rates soar—South Korea now has a rate of 1,940 cigarettes per person; in China the rate is 1,408; and in Brazil, 1,088, for example. In most developing countries, however, the rates are much lower: 764 cigarettes per person in Indonesia, 230 in Kenya, and 219 in Zimbabwe.[4]

Antismoking campaigns have recently gained support from some new sources. In the United States, smoking by parents of children with asthma and allergies has been used against them in child custody cases by non-smoking exspouses in more than a dozen states, and is expected to affect more cases in the future.[5] The argument will be bolstered by the Environmental Protection Agency's recent classification of secondhand smoke as a class A carcinogen and its report that this smoke annually causes 150,000–300,000 cases of bronchitis, pneumonia, and lower respiratory infections in infants and other illnesses.[6]

And the American Society of Clinical Oncologists recently called for cigarette taxes of as much as $3 a pack, saying that taxes may be much more effective at fighting cancer than medical treatment can be after disease develops.[7] Countries like France and Italy, which have been bastions of smoking, have joined in by banning tobacco in some public places.[8]

In other regions, tobacco consumption remains undiscouraged. Russia's appetite for cigarettes is so large that the supply annually falls 100 billion cigarettes short of demand. R.J. Reynolds International (RJR) is investing in new plants there to produce 22 billion cigarettes a year in a joint venture.[9] The British conglomerate BAT has signed letters of intent in Moscow to produce 700 billion cigarettes a year, seven times the size of its U.K. market.[10] The Philip Morris Company has agreed to pay $413 million for control of Tabak, a Czechoslovak cigarette manufacturer.[11] And similar investments are occurring in places like Kazakhstan and eastern Germany.[12]

Markets for foreign cigarettes have opened recently in South Korea, and may eventually in China.[13] Indeed, U.S. tobacco firms—despite a 15-percent drop in domestic cigarette consumption since 1986—have boosted production 5 percent to supply an expanding export market.[14] Since 1986, U.S. cigarette exports have gone from $1.3 billion to $4.2 billion.[15]

All this means that while smoking rates are going down among many groups of people, the damages cigarettes can cause lies ahead for others. Among Spanish women, for example, only 3 percent of those age 60 have the habit, but half the 20-year-olds smoke.[16] And if the share of Chinese women who smoke begins to approach that of men—70 percent—hundreds of millions more people will be at risk.[17]

WORLD CIGARETTE PRODUCTION, 1950–92

YEAR	PRODUCTION (billion)	PER CAPITA (number of cigarettes)
1950	1,686	660
1951	1,733	668
1952	1,780	676
1953	1,827	682
1954	1,874	687
1955	1,921	691
1956	1,968	695
1957	2,015	698
1958	2,062	700
1959	2,108	703
1960	2,150	708
1961	2,140	695
1962	2,191	699
1963	2,300	718
1964	2,402	733
1965	2,564	767
1966	2,678	784
1967	2,689	772
1968	2,790	785
1969	2,924	806
1970	3,112	840
1971	3,165	837
1972	3,295	854
1973	3,481	884
1974	3,590	895
1975	3,742	916
1976	3,852	926
1977	4,019	950
1978	4,072	946
1979	4,214	962
1980	4,388	985
1981	4,541	1,002
1982	4,550	987
1983	4,547	970
1984	4,689	983
1985	4,855	1,000
1986	4,987	1,010
1987	5,128	1,020
1988	5,266	1,030
1989	5,295	1,017
1990	5,453	1,029
1991	5,390	1,001
1992 (prel)	5,392	984

SOURCES: Dan Stevens, USDA, FAS, unpublished printout, November 7, 1991; data for 1950 based on U.S. trend; 1951–58 numbers simple arithmetic extrapolations; USDA, private communication, March 1993.

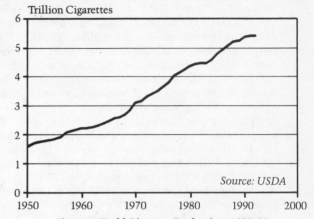

Trillion Cigarettes

Figure 1: World Cigarette Production, 1950–92

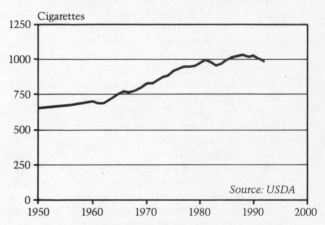

Cigarettes

Figure 2: World Cigarette Production Per Person, 1950–92

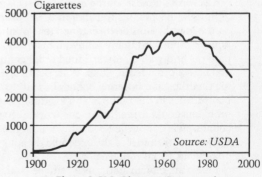

Cigarettes

Figure 3: U.S. Cigarette Consumption Per Adult, 1900–92

The number of official refugees in the world reached 18 million in 1992, an all-time high. (See Figure 1.) The number has grown steadily since 1976, when it stood at 2.8 million.[1] The burgeoning number of refugees—defined as people who flee their countries because of a well-founded fear of persecution due to political or religious beliefs or ethnic origin—is an indication that basic human needs are not being met despite improvements in modern engineering, communications, and technology.

Asia has the highest number of official refugees, with 8 million in 1990, an increase from just 180,000 in 1976. Africa is second, with 5.6 million, up from 1.2 million in 1976. North and South America are home to 2.7 million refugees, and Europe has fewer than 1 million.[2]

The rise may be due to accumulating stresses of recent decades, because most refugees flee long-term problems rather than sudden ones. War in Afghanistan, for example, has been by far the largest source of refugees worldwide, at about 6 million, and it represents 13 years of continued exile and displacements (though Afghanis are now slowly returning).[3] Refugees in the Sudan, Ethiopia, and Somalia suffer from year after year of ethnic conflicts, social disintegration, poverty, soil erosion, and deforestation.

The opening up of Eastern Europe, the former Soviet Union, and Albania, along with the collapse of Yugoslavia, will spur migration into Western Europe. Italy turned away 28,000 Albanians during one weekend in 1991.[4] In the future, North Africa appears likely to be Western Europe's largest source of asylum seekers.

In 1992, people in sub-Saharan Africa were on the march. Famine threatened tens of millions of them, and many followed historical patterns and walked toward food relief camps and better-provided regions. War, politics, ethnic rivalries, and faltering economies all played roles in the famines and exodus. Those problems could drive the official world refugee count upward, but they probably will not, because many or most of these people do not qualify as official refugees.

Receiving official status as a refugee (and, therefore, assistance) requires proof of well-grounded fear of war or of political, racial, or religious persecution, so many who flee their homes do not qualify. Those leaving an area because of crop failures or the loss of livelihoods are not counted, even if war exacerbated their plight. Nor are those who flee but do not cross national borders—they are considered a domestic problem. Yet they are thought to be greater in number than official refugees.[5] (See Figure 2.)

Because of these large numbers, unofficial refugees merit their own categories. People fleeing land degradation and the collapse of natural resource systems that provided livelihoods and food, or escaping pollution that threatened their health, now are being called environmental refugees by many people. Economic refugees are those fleeing poverty severe enough to threaten their lives and families. And "oustees" are people displaced by development projects such as large dams that flood village areas. Although the latter might sound like a small group, some estimates put the number in India alone at 10–20 million, as high as the number of official refugees worldwide.[6] Most of these new categories of refugees are domestic ones, because the people rarely cross national borders.

Displaced people are an indicator of future instability as well as past. Even after the refugees return home, the problems that forced them to leave seldom disappear easily. Those problems may show up in the form of migrations, but they really reflect more fundamentally an interplay among human rights, desperate poverty, war, and environmental degradation. Curing the symptom is not the same as curing the causes.

Ultimately, refugees are about security. They flee from insecurity of all kinds—environmental insecurity, personal insecurity, violations of human rights, armed conflict—and they exacerbate security concerns in both their old and their new homes. The least costly solution may involve a redefinition of what societies view as national security. Long-term personal safety, secure livelihoods, stable communities, and physical health offer the greatest hope of reducing the flow of refugees.

WORLD REFUGEES REGISTERED BY
U.N. HIGH COMMISSION, 1976–92

YEAR	REFUGEES (million)
1976	2.8
1977	3.3
1978	4.6
1979	5.7
1980	8.2
1981	9.8
1982	10.4
1983	10.9
1984	10.5
1985	11.6
1986	11.7
1987	12.2
1988	13.3
1989	14.7
1990	15.5
1991	17.2
1992 (prel)	18.0

SOURCE: UNHCR Washington Office,
private communication, March
19, 1993.

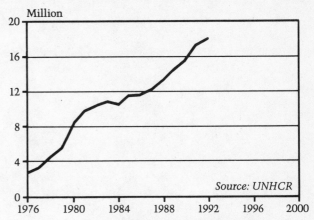

Figure 1: Official Refugees, World Total

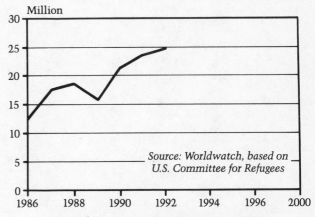

Figure 2: Estimated Number of People Forced from
Their Homes But Not from Their Countries, 1986–92

Part **TWO**

Special Features

Environmental Features

Water Scarcity Spreading   Sandra Postel

Although fresh water is a renewable resource, it is also a finite one. The water cycle makes available only so much water each year in a given location. That means supplies per person, a broad indicator of water security, drop as population grows. Thus per capita water supplies worldwide are a third lower now than in 1970 due to the 1.8 billion people added to the planet since then.[1]

One of the clearest signs of water scarcity is the increasing number of countries in which population has surpassed the level that can be sustained comfortably by the water available. As a rule of thumb, hydrologists designate water-stressed countries as those with annual supplies of 1,000–2,000 cubic meters per person. When the figure drops below 1,000 cubic meters (about 725 gallons per person a day), nations are considered water-scarce—that is, lack of water becomes a severe constraint on food production, economic development, and protection of natural systems.[2]

Today, 26 countries, collectively home to some 230 million people, fall into the water-scarce category. (See Table 1.) Many of them have very high population growth rates, so their water problems are deepening fast. For a country like Egypt, which gets practically no rainfall, water flowing in from upstream neighbors is a precious lifeline. Africa has the largest number of water-scarce countries, 11 in all, and by the end of this decade, four others will join the list.[3] By then, the total number of Africans living in water-scarce countries will climb to 300 million—a third of the continent's projected population.[4]

Nine out of 14 countries in the Middle East already face water-scarce conditions, making it the most concentrated region of water scarcity in the world. Populations in six of them are projected to double within 25 years, so a rapid tightening of supplies is inevitable. With virtually all Middle East rivers being shared by several nations, tensions over water rights are a potent political force throughout the region, and could ignite during this decade.

Although the population-water equation suggests where to expect trouble, numerous physical symptoms of water stress already exist—and not just in water-scarce countries, but in parts of water-wealthy ones as well. Among the most pervasive problems is that of declining water tables, which is caused by using groundwater faster than nature replenishes it. Overuse of groundwater is now ubiquitous in parts of China, India, Mexico, Thailand, the western United States, north Africa, and the Middle East.

Some of the most worrisome cases of unsustainable groundwater use involve "fossil" aquifers, underground reservoirs that hold water hundreds or thousands of years old and that receive little replenishment from rainfall today. Like oil reserves, these aquifers are essentially nonrenewable: pumping water from them depletes the supply in the same way that extractions from an oil well do. Farms and cities that depend on this water will eventually face the problem of what to do when the wells run dry.

In the United States, a large and important aquifer system in the High Plains, which contains the well-known Ogallala formation, has been undergoing depletion for several decades. Stretching from southern South Dakota to northwest Texas, the High Plains aquifer supplies about 30 percent of the groundwater used for irrigation in the United States.[5]

The most severe depletion has occurred in northwest Texas, where heavy pumping for irrigation began to expand rapidly in the forties. As of 1990, 24 percent of the Texas portion of the Ogallala had been depleted, a loss of 164 billion cubic meters—equal to nearly six years of the entire state's water use for all purposes.[6] As pumping costs rose and irrigation became uneconomical, the irrigated area in northwest Texas shrank rapidly, falling from a peak of 2.4 million hectares in 1974 to 1.6 million hectares in 1989, a drop of one third.[7]

In many regions, as demands continue to rise and as water supply projects get more difficult to build, water budgets are becoming badly imbalanced. China—with 22 percent of the world's people and only 8 percent of its fresh water—faces obvious water constraints.[8] The nation's predicament is particularly severe in and around Beijing, the important industrial city of Tianjin, and other portions of the North

China Plain, a vast expanse of flat, fertile farmland that yields a quarter of the country's grain.[9] Water tables beneath the capital have been dropping 1–2 meters a year, and a third of its wells have reportedly gone dry.[10] All told, some 100 Chinese cities and towns, mostly in the northern and coastal regions, have suffered shortages in recent years.[11]

In some cases, water problems stem directly from mismanagement and degradation of the land. When rain hits the earth, it either runs off immediately into rivers and streams to head back to the sea, soaks into the land to replenish soil moisture and groundwater supplies, or is evaporated or transpired (by plants) back into the atmosphere.

Land degradation, whether from deforestation, overgrazing, or urban development, shifts the proportion of rainfall following each of these paths. With reduced vegetative cover and soils less able to absorb and hold water, degraded land increases flash runoff and decreases seepage into the soil and aquifer recharge. As a result, less soil moisture and groundwater are available to draw upon during the dry season, and during the rainy season the rapid runoff intensifies flooding and soil erosion.

These examples by no means constitute a complete cataloging of the water problems evident in the world today. But together they illustrate some of the clearest signals of water stress. Shrinking groundwater reserves, falling water tables, increased flooding and droughts, and water budgets that are badly out of balance are tangible indications of unsustainable water use—a situation that, by definition, cannot continue indefinitely.

Adapted from
Last Oasis: Facing Water Scarcity,
W.W. Norton & Company,
1992

TABLE 1: WATER-SCARCE COUNTRIES, 1992[1]

REGION/COUNTRY	RENEWABLE WATER SUPPLIES PER PERSON (cubic meters)	POPULATION (million)	PROJECTED POPULATION SIZE AT STABILIZATION[2] (million)
Africa			
Algeria	730	26	78
Botswana	710	1	4
Burundi	620	6	32
Egypt	30	56	120
Kenya	560	26	125
Libya	160	4	36
Mauritania	190	2	14
Rwanda	820	8	65
Tunisia	450	8	18
Middle East			
Israel	330	5	10
Jordan	190	4	28
Kuwait	0	1	5
Saudi Arabia	140	16	89
Syria	550	14	66
United Arab Emir.	120	2	3
Yemen	240	10	110
Other			
Belgium	840	10	9
Hungary	580	10	10
Netherlands	660	15	14
Singapore	210	3	4

[1]Countries with per capita renewable water supplies of less than 1,000 cubic meters per year. Does not include water flowing in from neighboring countries. The table does not include six small, water-scarce countries with a combined population of 2.5 million: Bahrain, Barbados, Cape Verde, Djibouti, Malta, and Qatar. [2]World Bank projections, which show the level at which population will stabilize if recent fertility and mortality trends continue.
SOURCES: Population Reference Bureau, *1992 World Population Data Sheet* (Washington, D.C.: 1992); World Resources Institute, *World Resources 1992–93* (New York: Oxford University Press, 1992); World Bank, *World Development Report 1992* (New York: Oxford University Press, 1992).

Air Pollution Damaging Forests   Derek Denniston

After suffering from the cumulative effects of air pollution for decades, temperate forests in dozens of countries are now in decline. Air pollutants generated by the burning of fossil fuels for industry, transportation, and electricity are blanketing forests at an unprecedented rate and scale, placing them under severe stress. And tropical forests are starting to be affected, too.

In a 1991 survey of three quarters of Europe's forests, the U.N. Economic Commission for Europe and the European Community found that 22.2 percent were damaged—up from 20.8 percent in 1990. First surveyed in 1985, European forests over the past decade have shown "a deterioration in the majority of countries," according to the report.[1]

Scientists continue to search for the precise mechanisms of the forest decline, but most concur that air pollutants—including acid-forming sulfates and nitrates, gaseous sulfur dioxide, ozone, and heavy metals—along with natural stress factors are primarily responsible. Acting singly or together, air pollutants weaken trees in several ways.

Directly, they cause tree crowns to thin, as well as leaves and needles to yellow and drop prematurely from branches, leading to stunted growth or death.[2] Indirectly, acids in soils may leach away calcium, magnesium, and phosphorus—nutrients critical to tree growth and maintenance. Acidic imbalances also cause the thread-like tree roots to adsorb toxic soil solutions of aluminum and heavy metals. This soil leaching reduces forest growth, and may undermine the health of acid-sensitive forests for decades to come.[3]

Stressed by air pollutants, acidic and impoverished soils, or toxic metals, trees lose their resistance to natural events such as drought, pests, wind, or temperature extremes. Taken together, these direct and indirect pressures threaten not only future wood supplies, but the ability of forests to protect watersheds, stabilize soils, and harbor biodiversity.

According to the U.N. report, the hardest hit species overall has been the cork oak, with 43 percent "damaged" (defined as more than 25 percent loss of foliage). The United Kingdom

was hit hardest of all European nations, with 57 percent of its trees showing damage. Of the fir trees over 60 years old in Poland, 77 percent are damaged. Since the survey began, Eastern Europe has shown the largest increase in this category. The total area of damaged forests now covers about 475,000 square kilometers, an area larger than Germany.[4] (See Table 1.)

Researchers at the International Institute for Applied Systems Analysis (IIASA) in Austria calculated that about 75 percent of Europe's trees receive damaging levels of sulfur deposi-

TABLE 1: ESTIMATED FOREST DAMAGE IN EUROPE, 1991

COUNTRY	TOTAL FOREST AREA (thousand hectares)	SHARE DAMAGED (percent)
United Kingdom	2,200	57
Poland	8,654	45
Czechoslova-kia	4,491	41
Portugal	3,372	30
Russia	31,592	26[1]
Germany	9,828	25
Bulgaria	3,314	22
Switzerland	1,186	19
Finland	20,059	16
Romania	6,244	10
Spain	11,792	7
France	14,440	7
Others[2]	96,844	n.a.
Total[3]	214,016	22

[1]Conifer only. [2]Includes Austria, Belgium, Denmark, Estonia, Greece, Hungary, Ireland, Italy, Lithuania, Liechtenstein, Luxembourg, the Netherlands, Norway, Slovenia, Sweden, and Yugoslavia (excluding Croatia and Slovenia). [3]Does not include Byelorussia, Croatia, Latvia, Turkey, or Ukraine.
SOURCE: Worldwatch Institute, based on U.N. Economic Commission for Europe, Executive Body for the Convention on Long-range Transboundary Air Pollution, "Forest Condition in Europe: The 1992 Report," Geneva, September 14, 1992.

tion.[5] An IIASA study estimated that the deterioration of Europe's forests due to air pollution results in economic losses of $35 billion each year, roughly equivalent to half the gross national product of Hungary.[6] A four-year study found that the current rate of emissions is decreasing the annual timber harvest by 15 percent, equal to 83 million cubic meters.[7]

A similar study in the European region of the former Soviet Union concluded that air pollution there is reducing the harvest of logs by more than 13 percent annually, or 35 million cubic meters.[8] Forest health surveys in the Nordic countries are recording the preliminary symptoms of forest decline—crown thinning, needle loss, and yellowing—that were first observed 20 years ago in the severely damaged forests of Central Europe.[9]

In North America, no comprehensive surveys of forest damage have been done. What the United States has done is 14 years of research—in the most costly environmental study ever conducted there—to conclude that the link between air pollution and forest damage is uncertain, given the multiple stresses observed.[10] Some researchers claim the review process was politically manipulated by the electric utilities and paper industries to squelch evidence Congress could use to demand greater reforms under the 1990 Clean Air Act amendments.[11] Nonetheless, evidence is emerging of damage from airborne nitrogen oxides in the forests of the Great Smoky Mountains, the oak hickory forests of the Ohio River Basin, and possibly the southeastern pinelands and the Great Lakes region.[12]

Acid rain in the northeastern United States and southeastern Canada has caused sugar maples to lose their crowns and syrup production.[13] The high-elevation red spruce forests throughout the Appalachian mountains and the eastern United States have lower growth rates and increased mortality due to the prevalence of acidic cloud water.[14] And excessive ground-level ozone has been documented as the primary cause of the declining health of the Jeffrey and Ponderosa pines of southern and central California.[15]

The problem of air pollution damaging trees is no longer confined to the temperate forests

of industrial countries. As the world's biggest user of sulfur-rich coal, China is also witnessing forest damage due to air pollution, concentrated in the southern provinces of Guangdong, Sichuan, and Guizhou.[16] Acid rain now falls on 14 percent of the country and is estimated to have caused $2.8 billion in damage in 1991 to forests, farm crops, and buildings across the nation.[17] With coal combustion projected to increase by 35 percent during this decade, further damage seems certain.[18]

Most European efforts to date to curb air pollution have centered on mandating stricter uniform emission standards for motor vehicles, factories, and power plants. The regulations call for catalytic converters for cars and high-tech scrubbers for smokestacks.[19] But the IIASA study found that adopting even the most effective pollution control technologies available would still leave half of all forests receiving damaging levels of nitrogen oxide deposition and one quarter getting damaging levels of sulfur deposition—more than enough to continue reducing the long-term viability of European forests.[20]

Discussions in early 1993 on a new sulfur emissions protocol for Europe's Convention on Long-range Transboundary Air Pollution took a new approach by negotiating phases of pollution reduction to get emissions below thresholds of ecological tolerance, known as "critical loads."[21] Modelers of acid deposition in Europe have calculated that bringing sulfur and nitrogen oxide deposition levels below ecologically harmful levels will require a comprehensive restructuring of the existing energy system.[22]

The most obvious and affordable way to reduce emissions is to use energy more efficiently, especially in homes, vehicles, factories, and power plants. Shifting to wider use of natural gas will also be helpful, given that combustion of natural gas produces almost no sulfur and far less nitrogen oxide emissions than coal or oil do. Ultimately, only the transition from a fossil fuel to a renewable energy economy—based on solar, wind, geothermal, hydropower, and, eventually, hydrogen technologies—will achieve the needed dramatic reductions of virtually every major air pollutant.[23]

Many Marine Mammal Populations Declining   Ed Ayres

Population collapses and extinctions of the earth's plant and animal species are now taking place at several thousand times the natural "background" rate of biodiversity loss that has prevailed throughout the planet's biological history.[1] Losses of marine mammals—whales, dolphins, seals, manatees, and the like—constitute only a tiny portion of the overall devastation, but have caused particular concern because they serve as highly visible indicators of the difficulties other species, including humans, face. They are also of interest because they share much in common with us: they are at the top of their food chain, compete with humans for many of the same food sources, and may be affected by many of the same kinds of pollutants or environmental disruptions.

Public alarm has been particularly aroused by the growing frequency of such mysterious occurrences as the die-off of bottlenose dolphins off the U.S. Atlantic Coast in 1987–88, which may have cut the region's population in half; the sudden deaths of more than 14,000 seals in northern Europe the following year; and the highly publicized self-strandings of whales—sometimes whole schools at a time.[2] Of the 1,200 whale-beachings known to have taken place in the past two centuries, two thirds have occurred since the fifties.[3] Yet for all the concern these events cause, they represent only a small portion of the overall losses taking place in the marine mammal world.

Like human cultures, sea mammal populations have had widely varying fortunes over the past century of unprecedented change in the geophysical and biological environment. But it is noteworthy that in recent years many species have declined drastically in population, and some appear headed for extinction. (See Table 1.) Globally, most whales and porpoises are declining.[4] The blue whale, for example—the largest animal on earth—once numbered about 200,000 but is now estimated at fewer than 2,000. The humpback whale, once at 125,000, is now at about 10,000. The sei whale has dropped from 200,000 in preindustrial times to 25,000 today; the fin whale, from 470,000 to 110,000; and the right whale, from 200,000 to 3,000.[5]

For some species, global populations are unknown—but regional trends follow a similar pattern. Dolphins off the Pacific coast of Mexico and Central America have declined by about half since purse-seine nets (huge sieve-like traps) were intro-

TABLE 1: CHANGES IN MARINE MAMMAL POPULATIONS SINCE MID-CENTURY

SPECIES	PAST POPULATION[1]	RECENT POPULATION[2]
Declines		
Sei Whale	200,000	25,000
Fin Whale	470,000	110,000
Blue Whale	200,000	2,000
Humpback Whale	125,000	10,000
Right Whale	200,000	3,000
Bowhead Whale	120,000	6,000
Northern Sea Lion	154,000	66,000
Juan Fernandez Fur Seal	4,000,000	600
Hawaiian monk seal	2,500	1,000
Recoveries		
Gray Whale	10,000	21,000
Galapagos fur seal	near extinction	30,000
Antarctic fur seal	near extinction	1,530,000
Walrus	50,000	280,000
Dugong	30,000	55,000

[1]Late nineteenth to mid-twentieth century. [2]Late eighties to present.
SOURCES: National Oceanic and Atmospheric Administration (NOAA), Office of Protected Resources, *Marine Mammal Protection Act of 1972, Annual Report 1988–89* (Washington, D.C.: U.S. Department of Commerce, 1992); NOAA, *Our Living Oceans: The First Annual Report on the Status of U.S. Living Marine Resources* (Washington, D.C.: 1991); Ron Nowack, Office of Scientific Authority, U.S. Fish and Wildlife Service, Arlington, Va., private communication, January 1993.

duced in 1959 for yellowfin tuna fishing.[6] Although the problem was partially alleviated by the invention of a modified net allowing some dolphins to escape, some 20,000–50,000 dolphins are still drowned in the nets each year.[7]

Ironically, protections instituted to protect some marine mammals have increased pressure on others. In Japan, the national appetite for whale meat has heightened the demand for Dall's porpoise. Although the world's population of this animal is estimated at 2.2 million, Japanese hunters were killing 40,000 per year by 1988—considered by some marine biologists to be an unsustainable pressure on the species.[8]

Among the pinnipeds (sea mammals with four flippers), many species appear to be stable—but others are in sharp decline. The northern sea lion dropped from about 154,000 in 1960 to 66,000 in 1990.[9] The Juan Fernandez fur seal, once numbering 4 million worldwide, has declined to about 600.[10] And the decline can be extremely rapid: off the coast of Namibia, the seal population collapsed in just four years when overfishing depleted the animals' food supply. Whereas 54,000 seal pups survived in 1985, only 3,000 lived past 10 months of age in 1989.[11] In the Bering Sea, the Steller's sea cow was killed off within 27 years of its discovery by nonindigenous hunters.[12]

The causes of decline are many—most of them resulting from human activity. Some mammals are still targets for hunters. Many more are killed in "incidental take" when caught in fishers' nets.[13] Others, such as the bottlenose dolphins whose population collapsed along the northern Atlantic coast in 1987–88, may have been killed by pollutants.[14] In Europe, thousands of seals died of viral diseases in recent years—possibly because their immune systems were weakened by pollutants or other environmental disruptions.[15] And there are other human intrusions, as well. In Florida, the leading cause of death to manatees is collisions with boats.[16]

During the heyday of unrestricted commercial fishing in the latter half of the nineteenth century, many sea mammals were hunted nearly to extinction. Others thrived well into the twentieth century but came under increasing pressure after the first modern factory ship began processing whales at sea in 1925. Commercial whaling boomed in the thirties, with 46,000 whales—mostly blue whales—killed in the Antarctic region alone in the 1937–38 season. By the fifties, the blue whale was extinct commercially. Given protection in 1965, its population began to rebound.[17]

Similarly, at least four species of fur seals were decimated in the eighteenth and nineteenth centuries but have since recovered. The Antarctic variety—nearly extinct by 1900—now numbers about 1.5 million. In the North Pacific, the North American gray whale declined to about 10,000 in mid-century, but has since rebounded to about 21,000. Two other species of gray whale, however—in the Atlantic and West Pacific—have been lost.[18]

Protections have brought some stability to the world's overall population of marine mammals: the U.S. Marine Mammal Protection Act was passed in 1972, the 38-nation International Whaling Commission began a moratorium on commercial whaling in 1986, the European Council of Ministers banned purse-seining of marine mammals in 1992, and members of the United Nations resolved to ban driftnets by 1993.[19]

These protections appear precarious, however, in view of the growing appearance of conflict between short-term human economic demands and longer-term sustainability of marine activities. Both Norway and Iceland have said their economies depend on a resumption of commercial whaling, and the global whaling ban is under seige.[20]

More generally, the growing global demand for fish not only threatens continued attrition of mammals through injuries by boats or fishing gear, it also depletes the mammals' own food supplies. And even if fishing demands can be brought into line with the oceans' carrying capacity, the effects of other human-caused disruptions—notably pollution and atmospheric ozone depletion, which appears to be killing some of the phytoplankton that are a primary link in the marine food chain—have become growing problems.[21] Future trends among marine mammals may be a telling measure of stability in human society itself.

Economic Features

Wheat/Oil Exchange Rate Drops

Lester R. Brown

The world wheat/oil exchange rate, the bushels of wheat required to buy a barrel of oil, dropped in 1992—falling from just over 5.5 in 1991 to just under 4.5 in 1992. (See Table 1.) The price of oil was essentially unchanged, going from $18.30 in 1991 to $18.34 in 1992. But the world wheat price rose substantially, from $3.50 in 1991 to $4.11 in 1992.[1]

This exchange rate is of particular importance to the United States, which is both the world's largest exporter of grain and the largest importer of oil. The dramatic shift that began two decades ago set the stage for a massive, continuing outflow of capital from the United States, foreshadowing the conversion of the U.S. economy from one with a chronic trade surplus to one with a chronic deficit.

The global recession during 1992 weakened demand for oil and made it difficult for the Organization of Petroleum-Exporting Countries (OPEC) to curb production enough to raise prices, as many of its members wanted to do. In the absence of a major supply disruption, such as war, they are unlikely to be able to raise prices markedly in 1993.[2]

Drought-reduced harvests in northern Europe raised the need for wheat imports in that area. And part of the Canadian crop, heavily damaged by rain, had to be marketed as feedgrain, thus reducing the supply of the high-quality wheat typically imported into Europe to make bread. This damage to the Canadian wheat crop helps explain why the price of wheat went up even though the global harvest was 2.5 percent above the preceding year.[3]

In 1990, the year Iraq invaded Kuwait, the price of oil measured at the point of export from Saudi Arabia averaged $22.05.[4] At that time, the wheat/oil ratio was 5.9 bushels per barrel. This dropped in 1991 and again in 1992. For a country like the United States, which exports wheat and imports oil, this is a substantial improvement. But it is still a far cry from the period from 1950 to 1973, when a bushel of wheat could be exchanged for a barrel of oil in the world market.

Another factor affecting the price of oil is the growing competition from natural gas in a world increasingly concerned with air pollution. In various countries, gas is replacing oil for electric generation, for home heating and cooking, and, in a few instances, for transportation.[5] When cities begin to convert to natural gas, as for example Milan and Istanbul are doing, the demand for home heating oil and kerosene for cooking drops sharply.[6]

Another development affecting the position of oil is the adoption of taxes on carbon, energy, or gasoline. All of these tend to discourage the use of oil, making investments in efficiency more attractive. Such taxes are proving attractive to many governments for environmental and fiscal reasons and, in oil-importing countries, for balance of trade reasons as well.

The U.S. energy tax proposed by President Clinton in February 1993 taxes oil more than coal or gas, largely to reduce imports. The proposal calls for a tax on oil of 60¢ per million Btus, while both coal and natural gas would be taxed at 26¢ per million Btus. This would raise the price of oil by $3.47 per barrel when fully phased in during 1997.[7]

This tax will encourage investments in efficiency in such areas as transportation and home heating. Automobile buyers are expected to shift toward more-fuel-efficient vehicles in order to minimize or even offset the tax increase. The net effect is expected to be a reduction in oil imports of 350,000 barrels per year by 1997.[8]

The U.S. energy tax proposal is serving both fiscal and environmental goals. No tax is proposed on wind, solar, or geothermal energy.[9] Indeed, legislation passed in late 1992 would actually provide a tax rebate on investments in wind and solar electric generating facilities.[10] This will also discourage oil use in the United States.

Many governments in oil-importing countries realize that if they do not raise the prices of gasoline and other petroleum products through taxes, OPEC will raise them until they begin to reduce its share of the world oil market to an unacceptably low level. They know that the cost of producing oil in the Middle East—in Saudi Arabia, for example—is typically less than $2 per barrel.[11] By increasing

TABLE 1: THE WHEAT-OIL EXCHANGE
RATE, 1950–92

YEAR	BUSHEL OF WHEAT (dollars)	BARREL OF OIL	BUSHELS PER BARREL (ratio)
1950	1.89	1.71	1
1951	2.03	1.71	1
1952	1.93	1.71	1
1953	1.89	1.93	1
1954	1.98	1.93	1
1955	1.81	1.93	1
1956	1.84	1.93	1
1957	1.79	2.02	1
1958	1.62	2.08	1
1959	1.58	1.92	1
1960	1.58	1.50	1
1961	1.60	1.45	1
1962	1.75	1.42	1
1963	1.76	1.40	1
1964	1.84	1.33	1
1965	1.62	1.33	1
1966	1.71	1.33	1
1967	1.79	1.33	1
1968	1.71	1.30	1
1969	1.59	1.28	1
1970	1.49	1.30	1
1971	1.68	1.65	1
1972	1.90	1.90	1
1973	3.81	2.70	1
1974	4.89	9.76	2
1975	4.06	10.72	3
1976	3.62	11.51	3
1977	2.81	12.40	4
1978	3.48	12.70	4
1979	4.36	17.26	4
1980	4.70	28.67	6
1981	4.76	32.50	7
1982	4.36	33.47	8
1983	4.28	29.31	7
1984	4.15	28.25	7
1985	3.70	26.98	7
1986	3.13	13.82	4
1987	3.07	17.79	6
1988	3.95	14.15	4
1989	4.61	17.19	4
1990	3.69	22.05	6
1991	3.50	18.30	5
1992 (prel)	4.11	18.34	4

SOURCE: International Monetary Fund, *International Financial Statistics*, various years.

the tax on oil, governments of importing countries can capture part of the difference between the cost of production and the market price; otherwise, OPEC members will continue to get the lion's share of the difference.

For countries that export grain and import oil, the shift in the wheat/oil exchange rate from 5.5 bushels in 1991 to 4.5 in 1992 represented a substantial gain. For the members of OPEC, virtually all of whom import grain, this short-term shift was not to their advantage. Nonetheless, compared with the 1-for-1 ratio prevailing from 1950 to 1973, oil-exporting nations are obviously still much better off.

Cigarette Taxes on the Rise

Hal Kane

ealth officials in many countries are turning to higher taxes on cigarettes as a way to discourage smoking and reduce health care costs. For them, it is a triple-win situation. First, cigarette taxes bring in revenue. Second, they cut government spending on health care—yielding tens of billions of dollars in saved costs for national economies. And third, national economies enjoy greater productivity from workers who are healthier and require less sick leave, which yields the largest savings of all.

Every year, medical researchers uncover more ways in which cigarettes harm health. In 1992, tobacco use was linked to cataracts of the eyes in people smoking more than a pack of cigarettes a day.[1] Among children of smoking mothers, environmental tobacco smoke was found to cause anxiety, conflicts with other children, immaturity, antisocial behavior, and hyperactivity.[2] The U.S. Environmental Protection Agency officially classified environmental smoke as a class A carcinogen—grouping it with asbestos, benzene, and arsenic.[3]

Those diseases and disorders provide another reason for politicians' support for cigarette taxes—voters upset by smoking-related illnesses are in favor of them. Although tax hikes are usually met by public outcries, polls show cigarette taxes actually enjoy support, often even among smokers. A poll in Ontario by the Non-Smokers' Rights Association of Canada found support for tobacco taxes at 84 percent among nonsmokers and above 50 percent among smokers.[4] In the United States, Massachusetts voters adopted a 25¢ tax increase, doubling the state cigarette tax and making it the highest in the country, and New York is contemplating a 21¢ increase.[5] The Clinton administration seems to be pursuing a cigarette tax to reduce the federal deficit and cut health care costs. The potential to offset tobacco taxes by cutting income taxes, which otherwise discourage productive labor, also adds to the appeal of tobacco taxes.

Denmark's tax tops the world, at $3.68 per pack of 20 cigarettes, bringing the total price there to $4.33. (See Table 1.) Norway, Canada,

Sweden, Ireland, the United Kingdom, Finland, and Germany follow.[6] Other countries have not yet joined in. Spain, the United States, and Greece all charge far less than $1, despite having some of the world's highest smoking rates.[7] In developing countries, rates vary from year to year and from one blend of tobacco to another, though they are generally much lower than in industrial countries.[8]

The addictive nature of cigarettes, it turns out, does not diminish the effectiveness of reducing consumption by hiking prices. Raising cigarette prices cuts consumption directly. Fifteen studies reported by the U.S. Centers for

TABLE 1: SELECTED NATIONAL CIGARETTE TAXES AND PRICES PER PACK, JANUARY 4, 1993

COUNTRY	TAX PER PACK	PACK PRICE
	(dollars)	
Denmark	3.68	4.33
Norway	3.33	4.87
Canada	3.01	4.34
Sweden	2.87	3.93
Ireland	2.77	3.70
United Kingdom	2.55	3.41
Finland	2.45	3.32
Germany	2.11	2.92
New Zealand	1.81	2.67
France	1.58	2.08
Italy	1.11	1.54
Japan	1.05	1.75
Argentina	0.99	1.41
Greece	0.75	1.06
Taiwan	0.66	1.39
India	0.63	0.84
United States	0.56	1.89
Korea	0.46	0.76
Spain	0.37	0.60
Brazil	0.31	0.42
Philippines	0.24	0.44

SOURCE: Non-Smokers' Rights Association of Canada, Ottawa, private communication, January 4, 1993.

Disease Control (CDC) all concur: averaging out the findings, a 10-percent price rise caused a 4-percent drop in smoking among people over 20 years old.[9]

Even more important, cigarette taxes affect teenagers the most. About 90 percent of smokers start their habit before they are 20, which is also a time when they have low incomes. Teenagers who do not start smoking usually never will smoke. A 10-percent rise in cigarette price drops teen smoking a corresponding 10 percent.[10]

Canada's decisions over the last dozen years provide a precedent for cutting smoking through taxes. By raising its average tax from 38¢ in 1980 to $3.01 in 1992, the government lowered teen smoking by more than two thirds and smoking among adults by one half.[11] New Zealand took the same step: it nearly doubled the price of a pack between 1980 and 1991, and cigarette consumption dropped by almost half.[12]

The message sent by taxes is less ambiguous than ones sent by smoking education programs, public service announcements, and no-smoking sections of public buildings. For each of those, the message must be set against that of cigarette advertisements, which many people find compelling and glamorous. It is also offset by the 20–30 years that can separate smoking and the illnesses it causes. That lessens the urgency and directness that people would otherwise face when they consider the dangers of smoking. Taxes, on the other hand, are immediate—and their effects on the pocketbook are unambiguous.

The logic behind cigarette taxes is clear. When people smoke, they bill many of the costs to society. Government spending finances the health expenses incurred by smokers' decision to put themselves at risk, in the form of programs such as U.S. Medicaid and Medicare; employers pay for days missed from work; and consumers pay higher insurance premiums. People have the freedom to smoke, but not necessarily to have other people finance the results. Cigarette taxes make smokers pay their own costs.

For the United States, those amounts are estimated at $22 billion in government spending

on health care, and $43 billion in reduced productivity from missed days of work, according to a draft study from the Office of Technology Assessment.[13] The total, $65 billion, could be covered by a tax rate of about $2.50 per pack of cigarettes—less than in northern Europe. (As noted, the average U.S. tax is 56¢.)

U.S. health groups estimate that such a tax would reduce smoking rates enough to save nearly 2 million lives—more than lost in all U.S. wars combined.[14] As the higher tax lowered smoking rates, and thus cut economic damage, the revenue would slowly decline because cigarette sales would shrink.

Impressive as these dollar figures are, they greatly underestimate the value of attacking smoking-related disease because they do not include such immeasurable losses as the tragedy of early death and the disruption of families. If those were included, the value of cutting smoking would be even more evident.

People have long associated smoking with lung cancer, appropriately enough, as smoking-induced lung cancer causes about 112,000 deaths in the United States every year. But the death toll from smoking-related cardiovascular disease is greater. Strokes, aneurysms, heart attacks, hypertension, and other cardiovascular diseases attributed to smoking cause almost twice as many deaths as lung cancer. In addition, combined smoking-associated respiratory diseases cause over 80,000 deaths a year in the United States, mainly from chronic airways obstruction, pneumonia, influenza, bronchitis, and emphysema. Children's diseases and various cancers also add to the smoking-attributed death toll—a total loss that CDC calculated at 434,000 lives in the United States for 1988, the most recent year for which data are available.[15]

A 1992 study for the American Cancer Society estimated that about 2 million people a year die in the industrial world from tobacco-related illness. At present, more than 20 percent of all deaths in these countries are attributed to tobacco, and the figure is rising as researchers discover new links between cigarette smoking and health. During the nineties, cigarettes are expected to claim some 21 million lives in industrial countries.[16]

U.S. Seafood Prices Have Climbed   Hal Kane

As historical growth in the amount of food taken from the seas has diminished while the number of people and their demand for seafood continued to rise, logic dictated that seafood prices would rise. And they have. What was once an inexpensive source of high-quality protein in the United States is now one of the most expensive.

U.S. seafood prices were 40 percent higher in the early nineties than in 1950, after adjusting for inflation, with nearly all the rise coming since 1970 as more people fished. Prices of beef, by comparison, were down by more than one fourth over that period and those of poultry fell by two thirds.[1] (See Figure 1.)

What is ironic about the rising prices for seafood is that dramatic improvements in fishing technology during those years should have led to the opposite result. With chicken, for example, the decline in the U.S. price came despite almost a doubling in demand since the late sixties, because new technologies greatly expanded the output of broilers.[2] But with fish, a point was reached in many seas where species were harvested faster than they could reproduce, and stocks declined.[3]

Overfishing, limits on the growing supplies of seafood, and higher prices have all helped reshape the global diet. And seafood has become more desirable lately among consumers in the United States and other wealthy countries who like its low levels of fat and its taste. Now at almost 100 million tons a year, world consumption of fish exceeds that of beef and chicken combined; in some countries, fish provides most of the animal protein consumed.[4] But as prices rise, seafood may become less available to those who can no longer afford to pay for it.

In some developing countries, for example, the effect of higher seafood prices has been for the catch to leave local markets for those of industrial countries. The tonnage of seafood exports from developing countries has grown by three fourths in volume since 1981.[5] Until 1988, the European Community was self-sufficient in fish and shellfish (though some of that was caught off the coasts of developing countries), but rising consumption has now forced members of the Community to import.[6] In Japan, imports of seafood rose from $4 billion in 1985 to $10 billion in 1990.[7]

Thus, what happens to seafood prices in countries like the United States has implications for the consumption of seafood in many other regions as well. Growing income from fish exports may help the trade balances of indebted countries, but if it diminishes people's diets or leads to less employment, it will have done little for the poorest groups in those societies.

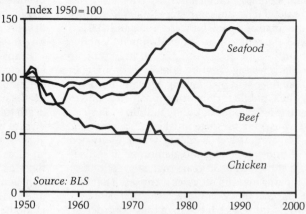

Figure 1: Changes in Real Price of Fish, Beef, and Chicken, 1950–92

The new economics of seafood is one that will touch jobs, national incomes, and natural resources. For example, in an effort to find new stocks, the United States is now bidding for fishing rights in previously off-limits Argentinean waters. Some Argentineans want to open those waters and sell the rights for cash; others want to fish the waters themselves and then sell the fish to the United States after processing in order to generate jobs and income for Argentina.[8] In other countries, the export of seafood may mean less access to it at home, even where traditional fishers have supported their families and their communities through the ages with fish.

As prices have risen, the attractiveness of fish farming has increased too. Worldwide, the controlled raising of fish in ocean pens and inland ponds or tanks has grown from 9.2 million tons in 1984 to 14.2 million tons in 1990.[9] That's about 14 percent of the total catch. Some people have even wondered if a "blue revolution" of aquaculture could do for food from the water what the Green Revolution did for food from the soil.

But aquaculture has its own problems. The easy spread of disease among fish kept in the tight quarters of a pen, the spread of that disease to wild stocks by fish that escape the pens, inbreeding and genetic weakening of natural stocks, pollution by fish wastes, and market stability are all matters of concern. Irish stocks of wild sea trout collapsed in 1989, for example, falling to less than 10 percent of their ordinary levels because of infestations of sea-lice, a parasite almost unheard of until salmon farming started in the area in the mid-eighties.[10] From Maine to Norway, production of salmon and other farmed fish has flourished and then been devastated, sometimes by disease, sometimes by competition from other producers.[11]

Despite these problems, the strong demand for fish and their rising prices can be expected to continue to make aquaculture a growing industry. Salmon farming in Chile, for example, which started in 1981, now accounts for 4.6 percent of world production.[12] And shrimp farming has expanded throughout Central America in the late eighties and early nineties.[13]

Although these aquacultural successes may help the supply situation, their effect on fish prices will be more ambiguous. Fish farmers compete with producers of beef, pork, poultry, and eggs for the same inputs—grain and soybean for feed, increasingly scarce fresh water, and valuable land. The cost of those inputs will raise the price of farmed fish, as will the costs of fighting disease among close-quartered stocks and the costs of pollution caused by aquaculture in coastal and inland areas.

Fish farming may draw feed and water away from the production of poultry, pork, and beef because it uses these resources more efficiently. Fish are cold-blooded, so they do not burn calories to keep themselves warm, and they need minimal muscle to move around in the water searching for food. Catfish, for example, one of the most efficient species, require only 1.75 pounds of feed to yield a pound of weight; by contrast, cattle in the feedlot require seven pounds of grain per pound of gain in the feedlot, pigs need roughly four pounds, and broilers, just over two.[14] Investment in aquaculture, in the long run, is likely to compete effectively with investments in other animal proteins.

Most of the world's natural rangelands and seas have already been exploited fully, so naturally occurring stocks of cattle, sheep, and goats, like those of fish, are already at their maximums. All future growth must come from grain-fed and water-supplied farming of animals, as has long been the case in most of the meat industry. Thus supplies of grain, water, and land constrain increased production of animal protein of all types.

If the efficiency of aquaculture allows it to compete effectively with meat production and to draw grain, water, and land away, then meat prices will rise because of shorter supply. Indeed, competition for resources among all types of animal protein could cause prices to rise together. Rising seafood prices may be only the first step into a new era during which the prices of many foods begin to head upward.

Social
Features

Literacy Gaining Slowly   Ed Ayres

In the past four decades, the number of adults who can read has increased by about 1.8 billion worldwide—a net growth of some 120,000 people a day.[1] This continuing improvement in global literacy—from 56 percent of the population in 1950 to about 74 percent today—represents encouraging progress.[2] But it also hides troubling disparities between industrial and developing nations and between men and women.

In 1970, some 94 percent of adults over age 15 were considered literate in industrial countries, compared with only 45 percent in the Third World.[3] Since then, literacy rates in the developing countries have gained ground impressively, climbing to 65 percent.[4] (See Figure 1.) Unfortunately, that still leaves 1.4 billion illiterate adults worldwide.[5] With population having grown even faster than literacy over most of the past three decades, the absolute number of people who cannot read is greater now than it was in the early sixties.[6]

As education programs proliferated in the developing world between 1985 and 1990, literacy finally began to gain on population growth, and the total number of illiterates worldwide fell by 2.4 million—the first time the number has actually declined.[7] At that rate of improvement, however, it would take 3,000 years for the number of illiterates to approach zero.[8] Furthermore, as the income gap between rich and poor nations is now widening rather than narrowing, maintaining even this rate of improvement may be difficult.

The disparity between male and female literacy is pervasive, cutting across economic and regional lines. In 1970, about 70 percent of the world's men were able to read, but only 54 percent of the women.[9] By 1990, both sexes had increased in overall literacy but the gap between the two had narrowed only slightly—by 2 percentage points.[10] At this rate, it would take more than 200 years for women to be as literate as men.

Even more disturbing is the fact that in some areas, the gender gap has actually widened. In Africa, while women's literacy climbed from 11 percent in 1962 to about 30 percent in 1985, the rate for men increased from 26 to 56 percent during the same period; thus the gender gap increased from 15 percentage points to 26. Since 1985, however, African women have closed the gap slightly.[11]

Illiteracy in industrial countries, while affecting a diminishing percentage of the population, appears to constitute a growing social problem. Because an increasing proportion of all jobs in these economies demand some facility in reading and writing, those who lack

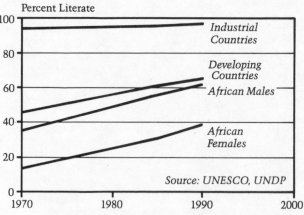

Figure 1: Adult Literacy, by Group, 1970–90

these skills are often mired in chronic unemployment and poverty.

In the Third World, literacy is not only a key factor in economic productivity but is a basic—though often disregarded—factor in the vicious cycle wherein uncontrolled population growth hastens environmental degradation, leading to still more intractable poverty. Efforts to stabilize population growth are unlikely to succeed without fundamental improvements in the status of women—including their rights and access to education.[12] Closing the literacy gap between men and women may thus be a significant measure of progress in human development.[13]

Regionally, there are large differences in literacy. Both overall and in terms of women's literacy, Africa is the most deprived of the continents. In 1990, less than a quarter of the adult population was literate in six countries in the world—all of them in Africa.[14] In 19 nations, 17 of them in Africa, the lifetime total schooling averaged less than one year for each adult. And in Burkina Faso, Djibouti, and Somalia, where fewer than one woman in five could read, it averaged less than three months.[15]

The functional importance of literacy to economic growth was formally recognized at a World Congress on Illiteracy held by UNESCO in 1965, which gave impetus to the establishment of numerous national programs.[16] Subsequent statistical surveys demonstrate a high correlation between literacy rates and income. In real per capita income, the 20 wealthiest countries in the world in 1990 included 18 of the 20 nations with the highest adult literacy scores. The only notable exception was Ireland, which ranked near the top in literacy but had modest per capita income, albeit higher than in most developing countries.[17]

Conversely, the greatest impoverishment is generally found in countries with the lowest levels of education and literacy. In the 30 nations with the lowest per capita gross domestic product (GDP) in 1990, the average adult had slightly more than one year of schooling.[18]

These general observations are confirmed by studies showing that when literacy is increased in a given country, productivity also rises. A study of 88 countries reported by the U.N. Development Programme found that a 20–30 percent increase in literacy produced gains of 8–16 percent in GDP. Another study concluded that "about a fifth of income inequality could be explained by educational inequality."[19]

Beyond economic motives, several other forces have propelled the movement that has led, during this century, from a world in which a minority of people could read to one in which three of every four people can. At the 1985 International Conference on Adult Education in Paris, literacy was identified as a fundamental human "right to learn."[20] The idea of literacy as a means to liberation has spread widely, and has clearly been a factor in the global movement toward democracy.

With few exceptions, low literacy is associated not only with greater poverty but with greater likelihood of political and social instability—resulting in still further sapping of national assets as resources are directed toward military security rather than social investment. A telling measure of this phenomenon is the ratio of soldiers to teachers, which is far higher in countries with low literacy and high poverty. It may be noteworthy that of 160 countries surveyed by the United Nations, the two with the highest soldier-teacher ratios were the very ones the U.S. government perceived a need for military intervention in during the past two years: Somalia and Iraq.[21]

Fertility Rate Decline Stalls Linda Starke

During the seventies, one of the encouraging developments in population trends was the reduction in the total fertility rate in several key countries, including the world's two largest nations—China and India. (This key demographic indicator measures the average number of children born to women in their childbearing years.) In China, the fertility rate dropped precipitously from 6.4 children per woman in 1968 to 2.2 in 1980. The decline in India was more modest, but still significant: from 5.8 children per woman in the period 1966–71 to 4.8 children in 1976–81.[1]

These trends helped slow the rate of world population growth from 2.1 percent in 1965–70 to 1.7 percent in 1975–80.[2] At that point, however, the decline in the number of children that women were having in these two population giants stalled.

In China, despite the most aggressive and least democratic population control program in the world, the fertility rate remained around 2.5 throughout much of the eighties as couples continued to want to marry young and to have two or more children. In India, the overzealous promotion of family planning by the ruling Congress Party through 1977 apparently backfired after their defeat, and progress toward lower birth rates ran out of steam.[3]

One important lesson from these experiences is that governments must do more than just supply contraceptives; they need to lower the demand for children by making fundamental changes that improve women's lives and increase their access to and control over money, credit, and other resources.

Many countries still register fertility rates above replacement level (see Table 1), which is generally 2.1 children per woman or basically two children per couple. The total fertility rate for the world as a whole in 1993 is 3.3, ranging from 1.8 in more developed nations to 4.4 in less developed ones (excluding China).[4] In a

TABLE 1. POPULATION SIZE, FERTILITY RATE, AND DOUBLING TIME, 20 LARGEST COUNTRIES, 1993

COUNTRY	POPULATION (mill.)	FERTILITY RATE (average no. of children/woman)	DOUBLING TIME (years)
Italy	58	1.3	3,466
Germany	81	1.4	654
Japan	125	1.5	217
Russia	149	1.7	990
United Kingdom	58	1.8	267
France	58	1.8	169
China	1,178	1.9	60
United States	258	2.0	92
Thailand	57	2.4	49
Brazil	152	2.6	46
Indonesia	188	3.0	42
Mexico	90	3.4	30
Turkey	61	3.6	32
India	897	3.9	34
Viet Nam	72	4.0	31
Philippines	65	4.1	28
Egypt	58	4.6	30
Iran	63	6.6	20
Nigeria	95	6.6	23
Pakistan	122	6.7	23

SOURCE: Population Reference Bureau, *1993 World Population Data Sheet* (Washington, D.C.: 1993).

number of countries, such as Brazil, Egypt, Indonesia, Mexico, and Thailand, fertility rates have been dropping as they did in the seventies in China and India. At the same time, a large group of developing countries has not yet entered the demographic transition.

The demographic transition occurs when both birth rates and death rates in a country drop from historically high levels to low ones that translate into a stable population—one that merely replaces itself with each new generation. Traditionally, although not always, death rates have declined first, following the spread of sanitation and improved health care overall. Rapid population growth often follows this first phase of the demographic transition, as the gap between fertility and mortality rates widens for a time. Eventually, however, fertility rates fall too.

At the moment, they remain high in a number of countries. The reasons for this are many and complex, and include unequal rights and opportunities for women as well as inadequate access to birth control. Whatever the reason, the effect is the same: 67 countries, home to 17 percent of the world population, are at best in the early stages of a transition to low fertility rates.[5] Most of them are in Africa and South Asia, and their populations are likely to double in 20–25 years.[6]

This is leading to a two-tiered demographic world that is every bit as worrying as the world of economic haves and have-nots. Countries such as Nigeria and Pakistan are finding it harder to keep up with the demand for food, health care, jobs, housing, and education than countries that are in the middle of the demographic transition.

As Shiro Horiuchi of Rockefeller University notes, "the demographic gap seems to overlap with a growing gap in economic development."[7] This gap has been growing for more than 20 years. In 1970, 34 percent of the world lived in countries with fertility rates below 5.5. Just five years later, thanks to the dramatic declines in India and especially China, the figure was 80 percent. It has not gained much since then, however, reaching 83 percent by 1985. More than three fourths of the significant de-

clines in fertility rates started in the 1965–70 period, and not many have begun since then.[8]

Even when a country does reach replacement-level fertility, its population can continue growing for decades. There is a built-in momentum created by all the people who have yet to enter their childbearing years. Indeed, the decline in the world's population growth rate stalled in the eighties in part because even in China, India, and other countries where fertility rates had been dropping, large number of people who had been born in the sixties reached childbearing age.[9] So even if couples had two or three children instead of five or six, as their parents did, the population would grow substantially.

For the world as a whole, if replacement-level fertility had been achieved in 1990 the population would continue to grow until it reached 8.4 billion in 2150 because of all the young people already alive.[10]

This built-in momentum obviously limits how quickly any country can stop population growth. Nevertheless, reaching replacement-level fertility is an all-important first step. The 67 countries that have not yet begun the demographic transition—nations in which invariably the government believes fertility levels are too high—could move in the right direction by providing the contraceptive and health care services that would help couples have only the number of children they desire.

Steven Sinding of the Rockefeller Foundation looked closely at the demographic goals (increased contraceptive usage or lower birth rates) of 12 developing countries. In 10 nations—including Bangladesh, Egypt, Kenya, and Pakistan—satisfying the unmet demand for family planning would bring fertility rates below government targets, by anywhere from 8 to 41 percent.[11] In estimating the global impact of such a development, he concluded that providing birth control to all who want it would bring fertility rates in the developing world from just below four children per women to just above three—halfway to replacement level.[12]

Military
Features

Nuclear Arsenal Decline on Hold   Michael Renner

The global nuclear arsenal peaked in 1988 and is now set for a dramatic decrease. The Strategic Arms Reduction Treaties (START I and II) will reduce the number of strategic offensive warheads held by the United States and the successor states to the Soviet Union from about 18,300 in 1991 to 6,500 by 2003.[1]

The "build-down" would thus be considerably faster than the buildup. But as dramatic as the agreed cuts seem, they would only return strategic warhead numbers to their 1968 level—the year the Nuclear Non-Proliferation Treaty was signed and the atomic powers pledged a serious move toward nuclear disarmament. By 2003, the remaining stockpile will still contain enough firepower to annihilate all life on earth.[2] In the meantime, work on new warhead designs and technologies, including so-called precision low-yield warheads, continues despite the cutbacks.[3]

In addition, implementing the planned cuts presents a major challenge. The obstacles are many. Can the Soviet heirs carry out the difficult and expensive job of dismantling nuclear weapons, or will the costs be judged prohibitive in an atmosphere of profound economic crisis? Will the turbulent politics in the Commonwealth of Independent States throw a wrench into plans for denuclearization? Can the dismantling of nuclear weapons be accomplished without clandestine diversion or theft of weapons-grade fissile materials? And can disarmament proceed in an environmentally safe manner?

START I was signed by the United States and the Soviet Union on July 31, 1991. By the end of that year, the Soviet state had been dissolved; of the new countries that surfaced in its place, four had strategic nuclear arms on their territories—Russia, Belarus, Kazakhstan, and Ukraine. (See Table 1.) It was unclear who was to be bound by the treaty's terms. The latter three states did not want to retain nuclear weapons, and the United States strongly preferred to continue dealing with only one opposite number in strategic arms matters—Russia.[4]

The Lisbon Protocol of May 1992 formalized the understandings that emerged after the Soviet breakup. Belarus, Kazakhstan, and

TABLE 1. STRATEGIC NUCLEAR WARHEADS, BEFORE AND AFTER START I AND II

COUNTRY	BEFORE START (1991)	AFTER START (2000/2003)[1]
	(number of warheads)	
United States	8,772	3,500
Former Soviet Union	9,537	3,000
of which:		
Russia	6,390	3,000
Ukraine	1,656	0
Kazakhstan	1,410	0
Belarus	81	0
France	436	384–768
China	324	> 400?
United Kingdom	96	256–512
World	19,165	7,540–8,180

[1]France, China, and the United Kingdom are not party to the START Treaties and their arsenals are therefore not subject to any internationally binding limits. Projected range of future warhead numbers for these three countries are rough estimates.
SOURCES: Graham Allison et al., eds., *Cooperative Denuclearization. From Pledges to Deeds* (Cambridge, Mass.: Harvard University, John F. Kennedy School of Government, 1993); Richard Fieldhouse et al., "Nuclear Weapon Developments and Unilateral Reduction Initiatives," in Stockholm International Peace Research Institute, *SIPRI Yearbook 1992: World Armaments and Disarmament* (Oxford: Oxford University Press, 1992); Dunbar Lockwood, Arms Control Association, Washington, D.C., private communication, February 23, 1993.

Ukraine committed themselves to eliminate all nuclear weapons on their territories (by moving them to Russia) within START's seven-year implementation period and to forswear any future acquisition and possession of nuclear arms. START I does not enter into force, however, until it and the Protocol have been ratified by all relevant parties. (And the follow-up START II agreement between the United States and Russia will not be implemented without START I coming into force.) So far, the United States, Russia, Kazakhstan, and Belarus have taken this step. Ukraine, the sole holdout, could tip the scales for or against nuclear disarmament.[5] But the dismantlement of nuclear arms in Russia itself appears to encounter numerous technical and political problems.[6]

In its Declaration of Sovereignty on July 16, 1990, Ukraine stated its intention to become nuclear-free. But more recently Ukraine's leaders have suggested that parliamentary approval of START I depends on the nation receiving both financial assistance to defray the costs of denuclearization and international guarantees of its security vis-à-vis Russia.[7]

The United States has offered Ukraine $175 million to help cover the expense of dismantling and transporting the weapons and of complying with other provisions of the START Treaty.[8] The cost is likely to be substantially larger, however. Ukraine says it wants up to $1.5 billion in compensation for giving up its nuclear weapons.[9]

Both the Russian and the U.S. government have offered Ukraine unspecified security assurances against foreign attack, to come into effect after Ukrainian ratification of START I and the Nuclear Non-Proliferation Treaty.[10] These verbal pledges may not be enough to assuage Ukrainian apprehension over Moscow's intentions, however, as a variety of Russian leaders have questioned Ukraine's sovereignty and the two countries remain divided over possession of the Crimea region and control of the former Soviet Black Sea fleet.[11] Although only a few parliamentarians want to renege on Ukraine's commitment and retain nuclear weapons, the majority nervously perceives that, as *New York Times* reporter Serge

Schmemann put it, "without its inherited nuclear might, Ukraine might lose its last claim to attention."[12]

Once this immediate question is resolved, additional problems loom. The START Treaties contain elaborate rules on how many and what kinds of weapons may be retained; extensive notification, inspection, and verification arrangements to ensure compliance with all treaty provisions; and detailed guidelines on how weapons above agreed limits may be cut up, crushed, burned, or otherwise eliminated. But the accords say nothing about what to do with the withdrawn warheads and the fissionable materials—plutonium and highly enriched uranium (HEU)—within them. By helping Moscow dismantle and store its nuclear weapons, the U.S. government may derive a measure of confidence that denuclearization in Russia remains on track (though Moscow is understandably reluctant to permit direct U.S. involvement in the process). But Russia has no reciprocal rights, and the rest of the world is entirely excluded from this process.[13]

After nuclear weapons are dismantled, the question is, What should be done with the stocks of plutonium and HEU? How can we "dispose" of these dangerous, long-lived substances? An acceptable method must make diversion of such materials difficult or impossible, make it difficult or impossible to return these materials to a form suitable for weapons, be affordable, and meet at least minimum safety and environmental standards.[14]

For decades, the cold war impeded any real progress toward denuclearization. Now that its end permits a substantial shrinking of the doomsday arsenals, the world has discovered that it may be as hard to dismantle the systems as it was to overcome political barriers to doing so.

U.N. Peacekeeping Surges
Michael Renner

When U.N. peacekeepers were awarded the Nobel Peace Prize in 1988, Secretary-General Javier Pérez de Cuéllar noted that for the first time in history "military forces have been employed internationally not to wage war, not to establish domination and not to serve the interests of any power or group of powers."[1] In the first four decades of U.N. peacekeeping, only 14 operations were undertaken. In recent years, however, the Blue Helmets have been inundated with requests for their services.[2]

The past five years have registered as many new operations as during the previous four decades—including the three largest ever undertaken.[3] (See Table 1.) Two factors explain this heightened demand: Stalemate, exhaustion, and war weariness have driven many combatants to embrace the U.N. as a peacemaker. And with the end of the cold war the superpowers pressured governments they had supported to make concessions in order to settle long-standing disputes.

Reflecting operations that are both larger in number and more ambitious in nature, annual U.N. peacekeeping outlays have risen sharply—from less than $233 million in 1987 to some $1.4 billion in 1992.[4] Expenditures are likely to rise even higher in 1993. Between 1990 and 1992, the number of people participating in these operations rose from 10,500 to more than 50,000.[5] This number is set to expand dramatically: some 31,000 peacekeepers are being

deployed in Somalia, and thousands more might be dispatched to Bosnia.[6] Since 1948, more than 650,000 people—military, police, and civilian personnel—have served in peacekeeping missions at one time or another.[7]

Traditionally, U.N. peacekeeping operations focused narrowly on conflict containment—monitoring borders and buffer zones after cease-fires have been signed, and preventing armed incursions or illegal arms flows across borders. But now they are moving beyond these tasks. Missions are more complex and ambitious, and are increasingly engaged not just in keeping the peace but in making it: supervising the disarming or disbanding of armed factions, establishing protected areas, monitoring elections and human rights rec-

TABLE 1. BUDGETS AND PERSONNEL OF RECENT U.N. PEACEKEEPING OPERATIONS

U.N. OPERATION	DURATION	BUDGET[1] (million dollars)	PERSONNEL[2]
Afghanistan/Pakistan	1988–90	7	50
Iran/Iraq	1988–91	9	750
Angola	1989–92[3]	110	298
Namibia	1989–90	410	6,150
Nicaragua	1989–90	2	494
Central America	1989–92	26	625
Haiti	1990	5	312
El Salvador	1991–92	70	530
Iraq/Kuwait	since 1991	67	353
Western Sahara	since 1991	59	332[4]
Cambodia	since 1991	1,700	18,901[5]
Croatia/Bosnia/Macedonia	since 1992	607	22,063[6]
Somalia	since 1992	1,550[7]	30,800
Mozambique	since 1993	332	7,500

[1]UN peacekeeping operations are not budgeted on a fiscal or calendar year basis but for a period of time that can be longer or shorter than a year. The figures here represent assessed budgets during 1992 for ongoing operations; for operations terminated in earlier years, the value for roughly the last active year is given. [2]At year-end 1992. [3]Mission may be extended, given the renewed outbreak of civil war. [4]Eventual full strength: 2,700. [5]Eventual full strength: 22,000. [6]Of whom about 7,500 in Bosnia; force in Bosnia may be boosted to 20,000 or more. [7]One-year cost estimate for a force to be deployed by May 1993.
SOURCE: Worldwatch Institute, based on numerous sources.

ords, repatriating refugees, and even—in the case of Cambodia—temporarily taking over the administration of an entire nation torn by war in order to facilitate the rebuilding of institutions and infrastructures, and thus the rebirth of civilian society.

The United Nations finds itself increasingly drawn into mediating and conciliating not only international but also internal conflicts, and facilitating political transitions. Most of the missions begun since 1988, including those in El Salvador, Namibia, and Cambodia, were charged with helping to resolve domestic conflicts and the transition to more democratic political systems.[8]

Although Article 2 of the U.N. Charter specifies that the United Nations is not authorized "to intervene in matters which are essentially within the domestic jurisdiction of any state," the distinction between internal and international affairs is being blurred for at least two reasons. First, civil strife within a country may have repercussions beyond its borders, either because outside powers are drawn into the conflict or because streams of refugees threaten to destabilize neighboring countries. Second, television images beamed around the world of massive human suffering caused by savage fighting or government repression in places like Iraq, Haiti, Somalia, and Bosnia have fed the demand for humanitarian intervention. One argument gaining support is that the protection of human rights in such cases should supersede the principle of national sovereignty.[9]

The future may bring even greater U.N. involvement in supervising the settlement of internal conflicts, because the vast majority of violent disputes today are not conventional wars between nations but domestic ethnic and political conflicts. Although important precedents are being set, the involvement of the United Nations in internal affairs raises difficult issues: such domestic involvement is far from universally accepted, particularly among governments of developing countries that suspect humanitarian relief efforts may simply be a convenient pretext for old-style intervention.[10]

Having evolved through improvisation, the current system is handicapped in a number of ways. One problem is that many member governments fail to pay their fair share. Total unpaid peacekeeping assessments stood at $645 million at the end of 1992.[11]

Furthermore, peacekeeping forces are created for specific missions only, and composed of contingents of national armed forces made available by governments voluntarily. Thus the U.N.'s ability to assemble and dispatch a force swiftly—to prevent a smoldering conflict from erupting into hostilities—is severely compromised.[12]

The experiences of the Iraq-Kuwait crisis and the devastation wrought by civil wars in the former Yugoslavia, Somalia, and other places have led a number of observers to conclude that only international military intervention could end these tragedies. If the United Nations is given the capability to become involved early in conflict resolution—before large-scale violence has occurred—the likelihood that force will have to be used in peacekeeping and peacemaking efforts will be lowered.

NOTES

OVERVIEW: AN AGE OF DISCONTINUITY

1. Royal Society of London and the U.S. National Academy of Sciences, *Population Growth, Resource Consumption, and a Sustainable World* (London and Washington, D.C.: 1992).
2. Union of Concerned Scientists, *World Scientists' Warning to Humanity* (Washington, D.C.: 1992).

GRAIN PRODUCTION RISES

1. U.S. Department of Agriculture (USDA), *World Grain Situation and Outlook*, Washington, D.C., February 1993.
2. Ibid.
3. USDA, *World Grain Database* (unpublished printout) (Washington, D.C.: 1992).
4. Ibid.
5. U.N. Food and Agriculture Organization (FAO), *Food Outlook*, Rome, October 1992; FAO, *Food Outlook*, Rome, February 1993.
6. FAO, October 1992, op. cit. note 5.
7. Ibid.
8. Marlise Simons, "Winds Toss Africa's Soil, Feeding Lands Far Away," *New York Times*, October 29, 1992.
9. USDA, Economic Research Service, *Western Europe Agriculture and Trade Situation and Outlook*, Washington, D.C., December 1992; FAO, October 1992, op. cit. note 5.
10. USDA, *World Agricultural Production*, Washington, D.C., August 1992.
11. USDA, *World Grain Situation and Outlook*, Washington, D.C., October 1992 and November 1992.
12. USDA, *World Agricultural Production*, Washington, D.C., December 1992.

13. FAO, October 1992, op. cit. note 5.
14. See pp. 40-43 for details on the trends mentioned in this paragraph.

SOYBEAN HARVEST SETS RECORD

1. U.S. Department of Agriculture (USDA), *World Oilseed Situation and Outlook*, Washington, D.C., February 1993.
2. Ibid.
3. All data in this paragraph from USDA, *World Soybean Database* (unpublished printout) (Washington, D.C.: 1992).
4. Ibid.
5. USDA, *Oil Crops: Situation and Outlook Report*, Washington, D.C., January 1993; USDA, op. cit. note 3.
6. USDA, *Agricultural Statistics 1992* (Washington, D.C.: U.S. Government Printing Office, 1992).
7. USDA, January 1993, op. cit. note 5.
8. USDA, op. cit. note 3.
9. USDA, January 1993, op. cit. note 5.
10. USDA, *World Grain Database* (unpublished printout) (Washington, D.C.: 1992).
11. USDA, op. cit. note 3.
12. Harold Dregne et al., "A New Assessment of the World Status of Desertification," *Desertification Control Bulletin* (U.N. Environment Programme), No. 20, 1991.

MEAT PRODUCTION UP SLIGHTLY

1. U.N. Food and Agriculture Organization (FAO), *1948-85 World Crop and Livstock Statistics* (Rome: 1987); FAO, *FAO Production Yearbook* (Rome: vari-

ous years); FAO, *Food Outlook*, Rome, February 1993.

2. FAO, February 1993, op. cit. note 1.

3. Ibid.

4. Data for red meat are from U.S. Department of Agriculture (USDA), *World Agricultural Production*, Washington, D.C., March 1993; poultry meat data are from USDA, *World Poultry Situation*, Washington, D.C., August 1992.

5. USDA, March 1993 and August 1992, op. cit. note 4.

6. USDA, *World Agricultural Production*, Washington, D.C., October 1992.

7. Ibid.

8. UDSA, *World Agricultural Production*, Washington, D.C., January 1993.

9. Ibid.

10. Ibid.

11. USDA, Economic Research Service (ERS), *Former USSR Update: Agriculture and Trade Report*, Washington, D.C., March 3, 1993.

12. H. Dregne et al., "A New Assessment of the World's Status of Desertification," *Desertification Control Bulletin* (U.N. Environment Programme), No. 20, 1991.

13. Feed-to-poultry conversion ratio derived from data in Robert V. Bishop et al., *The World Poultry Market—Government Intervention and Multilateral Policy Reform* (Washington, D.C.: USDA, 1990); conversion ratio for grain to beef based on Allen Baker, Feed Situation and Outlook staff, ERS, USDA, Washington, D.C., private communication, April 27, 1992; poultry data from Linda Bailey, Livestock and Poultry Situation staff, ERS, USDA, Washington, D.C., private communication, April 27, 1992, and from various issues of *Feedstuffs*; pork data from Leland Southard, Livestock and Poultry Situation and Outlook staff, ERS, USDA, Washington, D.C., private communication, April 27, 1992.

FISH CATCH NO LONGER GROWING

1. U.N. Food and Agriculture Organization (FAO), Rome, private communication, March 23, 1993.

2. Ibid.; World Resources Institute (WRI), *World Resources 1992–93* (New York: Oxford University Press, 1992).

3. FAO, *Yearbook of Fishery Statistics: Catches and Landings* (Rome: various years); 1989-91 data from FAO, op. cit. note 1.

4. David Gardner, "One Fifth of EC Fishing Fleet Hangs in Balance," *Financial Times*, October 20, 1992.

5. Bernard Simon, "Canada Set to Impose Ban on Atlantic Cod Fishing," *Financial Times,* July 7, 1992; Bernard Simon, "Canada Welcomes EC Fishing Curb, With Reservations," *Financial Times,* June 3, 1992.

6. "Iceland Faces Call for 40% Cut in Cod Catch," *Financial Times,* June 3, 1992.

7. Mike Griffin, "Some Very Fishy Business," *South,* August 1991; "Minister Says Fishing Policies Beginning To Show Results," South African Press Association, April 9, 1992, reprinted in *JPRS Report: Environmental Issues,* May 22, 1992.

8. "Fishing Limits in the Pacific," *Wall Street Journal,* October 29, 1992.

9. Michael Satchell, "The Rape of the Oceans," *U.S. News & World Report,* June 22, 1992.

10. Ibid.; Bryan Hodgson, "Hard Harvest on the Bering Sea," *National Geographic,* October 1992.

11. WRI, op. cit. note 2.

12. Ibid.

13. Testimony of Dr. Susan Weiler, Executive Director, American Society of Limnology and Oceanography, Department of Biology, Whitman College, Walla Walla, Wash., before Hearing on Global Change Research: Ozone Depletion and its Impacts, U.S. Senate, Committee on Commerce, Science, and Transportation, November 15, 1991.

14. FAO, op. cit. note 3.

GRAIN STOCKS INCREASE

1. U.S. Department of Agriculture (USDA), *World Grain Situation and Outlook*, Washington, D.C., February 1993.

2. Ibid.

3. Ibid.

4. International Monetary Fund, *International Financial Statistics Yearbook* (Washington, D.C.: various years).

5. USDA, op. cit. note 1.

6. Ibid.

7. USDA, *World Grain Situation and Outlook*, Washington, D.C., November 1992.

8. U.N. Food and Agriculture Organization (FAO), *Food Outlook*, Rome, October 1992.

9. USDA, *World Agricultural Production*, Washington, D.C., April 1992.

10. World Bank, *World Development Report 1992* (New York: Oxford University Press, 1992).

11. FAO, op. cit. note 8; FAO, *Food Outlook*, Rome, February 1993.

GRAIN USED FOR FEED UNCHANGED

1. U.N. Food and Agriculture Organization (FAO), *Food Outlook,* Rome, March 1993.
2. U.S. Department of Agriculture (USDA), *World Grain Situation and Outlook,* Washington, D.C., February 1993.
3. USDA, *World Grain Database* (unpublished printout) (Washington, D.C.: 1992).
4. FAO, *Food Outlook,* Rome, November 1992.
5. J.S. Sarma, *Cereal Feed Use in the Third World: Past Trends and Projections to 2000,* Research Report 57 (Washington, D.C.: International Food Policy Research Institute, 1992).
6. USDA, op. cit. note 3.
7. Ibid.
8. Ibid.
9. Ibid.
10. Ibid.
11. USDA, Economic Research Service, *Western Europe Agriculture and Trade Situation and Outlook,* Washington, D.C., December 1992.
12. USDA, op. cit. note 3.
13. Ibid.
14. Ibid.
15. Ibid.

GRAIN AREA UNCHANGED

1. U.S. Department of Agriculture (USDA), *World Grain Situation and Outlook,* Washington, D.C., February 1993.
2. Ibid.
3. Ibid.
4. Lester R. Brown, "Breakthrough on Soil Erosion," *World Watch,* May/June 1988; Peter Weber, "U.S. Farmers Cut Soil Erosion by One Third," *World Watch,* July/August 1990.
5. Lester R. Brown and John Young, "Feeding the World in the Nineties," in Lester R. Brown et al., *State of the World 1990* (New York: W.W. Norton and Company, 1990).
6. Annual population increase from Center for International Research, U.S. Bureau of the Census, Washington, D.C., private communication, March 26, 1993.
7. Calculated using world grain yield data from USDA, op. cit. note 1.
8. USDA, *China: Agricultural and Trade Report,* Washington, D.C., various years.

9. USDA, *World Grain Database* (unpublished printout) (Washington, D.C.: 1992).

FERTILIZER USE FALLS AGAIN

1. International Fertilizer Industry Association (IFA), *Fertilizer Consumption Report* (Paris: 1992).
2. U.S. Department of Agriculture (USDA), *Former USSR Agriculture and Trade Situation and Outlook,* Washington, D.C., May 1992.
3. USDA, *World Grain Database* (unpublished printout) (Washington, D.C.: 1992).
4. Sandra Postel, *Last Oasis: Facing Water Scarcity* (New York: W.W. Norton and Company, 1992).
5. From 1950 to 1980, U.S. fertilizer use climbed dramatically as yields responded to the application of additional fertilizer, but the failure of fertilizer use to increase at all during the eighties, even where commodity prices are favorable, indicates that yields are no longer very responsive to additional fertilizer. See Duane Chapman and Randy Barker, *Resource Depletion, Agricultural Research, and Development* (Ithaca, N.Y.: Cornell University, 1987).
6. USDA, *USSR Agriculture and Trade Situation and Outlook,* Washington, D.C., May 1991; IFA, op. cit. note 1.
7. USDA, *China: Agricultural and Trade Report,* Washington, D.C., various issues.
8. IFA, op. cit. note 1; U.N. Food and Agriculture Organization (FAO), *Fertilizer Yearbook* (Rome: various years).
9. FAO, *FAO Production Yearbooks* (Rome: various years); FAO, op. cit. note 8; IFA, op. cit. note 1.
10. USDA, *World Grain Situation and Outlook,* Washington, D.C., various years; FAO, op. cit. note 8.
11. USDA, op. cit. note 3; FAO, op. cit. note 8.
12. FAO, op. cit. note 8.
13. USDA, op. cit. note 3.
14. "Fertilizer Firms' Hopes for Turnaround Are Frustrated," *Wall Street Journal,* December 11, 1992; Ashok Gulati and G. D. Kalra, "Fertilizer Subsidy: Issues Related to Efficiency," *Economic and Political Weekly,* March 28, 1992.

OIL PRODUCTION STEADY

1. "Worldwide Crude Oil and Gas Production," *Oil & Gas Journal,* March 8, 1993.
2. British Petroleum, *BP Statistical Review of World Energy* (London: 1992).
3. "Worldwide Crude Oil and Gas Production," op. cit.

135

note 1; American Petroleum Institute (API), *Basic Petroleum Data Book* (Washington, D.C.: 1992).

4. "Worldwide Crude Oil and Gas Production," op. cit. note 1; API, op. cit. note 3.

5. "Worldwide Crude Oil and Gas Production," op. cit. note 1.

6. Ibid.

7. Ibid.

8. Worldwatch Institute estimate based on Tom Boden, Oak Ridge National Laboratory, Oak Ridge, Tenn., private communication and computer database, July 28, 1992.

9. "Oil Leakage Off Spain Exceeds Alaska Spill," *New York Times,* December 14, 1992.

10. Sanjoy Hazarika, "India Appeals for Help to Clean Up Major Oil Spill," *New York Times,* January 31, 1993; Kieran Cooke, "Malaysia's Disaster Warnings Go Unheeded in Strait of Malacca," *Financial Times,* January 26, 1993.

11. Deborah Hargreaves, "Unsung Heroes of the Sea," *Financial Times,* January 13, 1993.

12. "Russian Oil and Gas Pipelines Plagued by Accidents," *Oil & Gas Journal,* February 15, 1993.

13. Ibid.

14. Ibid.

15. Motor Vehicle Manufacturers Association, *World Motor Vehicle Data,* 1992 ed. (Detroit, Mich.: 1992).

WIND GENERATING CAPACITY EXPANDS

1. Paul Gipe, American Wind Energy Association, Tehachapi, Calif., March 30, 1993.

2. Ibid.; British Petroleum, *BP Statistical Review of World Energy* (London: 1993).

3. "The Quixotic Technology," *The Economist,* November 14, 1992; "Europe Gets Clean Away," *Wind Power Monthly,* September 1992.

4. Gipe, op. cit. note 1.

5. Andrew Garrad, *Wind Energy in Europe: Time for Action* (Rome: European Wind Energy Association, 1991).

6. American Wind Energy Association, *1992 Wind Technology Status Report* (Washington, D.C.: 1992).

7. David C. Walters, "New Technology Puts Wind Power on Par With Traditional Fuels," *Christian Science Monitor,* March 1, 1993.

8. Paul Gipe, American Wind Energy Association, Tehachapi, Calif., December 8, 1992.

9. Nicholas Lenssen, "California's Wind Industry Takes Off," *World Watch,* July/August 1990.

10. Derek Denniston, "Europe Catches the Wind," *World Watch,* May/June 1993.

11. Gipe, op. cit. note 8.

12. Denniston, op. cit. note 10.

13. George Stein, "Big Plan in Ukraine to Harvest the Wind," *San Francisco Examiner,* December 11, 1992; "Ukraine Emerges as the Next Great Market," *Wind Power Monthly,* February 1993; Jeff Pelline, "Bay Firm to Supply Windmills to Speed Chernobyl Closure," *San Francisco Chronicle,* February 19, 1993.

14. Ruth Caplan, "Losses and Gains in Energy Bill: Overview," *Power Line,* November/December 1992.

15. Robert D. Hershey, Jr., "Indirect Effects of the Energy Tax," *New York Times,* February 20, 1993.

16. *U.S. Wind Power Monthly* (various issues).

NUCLEAR POWER AT VIRTUAL STANDSTILL

1. Installed nuclear capacity is defined as reactors connected to the grid as of December 31, 1992, and is based on a data base at Worldwatch Institute and on Greenpeace International, WISE-Paris, and Worldwatch Institute, *The World Nuclear Industry Status Report: 1992* (London: 1992).

2. Worldwatch data base, compiled from statistics from the International Atomic Energy Agency and press reports.

3. "World List of Nuclear Power Plants," *Nuclear News,* March 1993; International Atomic Energy Agency, *Nuclear Power Reactors in the World* (Vienna: 1992); Worldwatch Institute data base.

4. Worldwatch Institute estimate based on data base.

5. "Finnish Nuclear Suffers Setback as MPs Vote Against New Plant," *European Energy Report,* November 13, 1992.

6. "EdF Orders Reactor Covers," *European Energy Report,* February 5, 1993; Howard LaFranchi, "French Lead Europe in Reactors and Power Generation," *Christian Science Monitor,* February 24, 1993.

7. U.S. Department of Energy, Energy Information Administration, *Commercial Nuclear Power* (Washington, D.C.: U.S. Government Printing Office, 1990).

8. "Canadian Nuclear Industry Expects Orders to Increase," *Multinational Environmental Outlook,* January 23, 1990.

9. Suzanne McGee, "Ontario Hydro Will Reduce Its Budget for Capital Spending to Cut Power Costs," *Wall Street Journal,* October 21, 1992.

10. Vladimir Chernousenko, *Chernobyl: Insight from the Inside* (New York: Springer Verlag, 1991); Keith Baverstock et al., "Thyroid Cancer After Chernobyl," *Nature,* September 3, 1992.

11. Greenpeace International, WISE-Paris, and Worldwatch Institute, op. cit. note 1.

12. Lydia Popova, Socio-Ecological Union, Moscow, private communication, January 29, 1993.
13. Greenpeace International, WISE-Paris, and Worldwatch Institute, op. cit. note 1; "World Status: A Grid for East Asia," *Energy Economist,* February 1992; David E. Sanger, "Japanese May Cut Atomic Shipments," *New York Times,* November 13, 1992.
14. Gregg M. Taylor, "Kepco Plans 18 More Reactors by 2006," *Nuclear News,* November 1992; Chung-Taek Park, "The Experience of Nuclear Power Development in the Republic of Korea," *Energy Policy,* August 1992.
15. Gregg M. Taylor, "Taipower Resumes Project; Improves Operating Plants," *Nuclear News,* October 1992.
16. Greenpeace International, WISE-Paris, and Worldwatch Institute, op. cit. note 1.
17. Robert Johnson and Ann de Rouffignac, "Nuclear Utilities Face Immense Expenses in Dismantling Plants," *Wall Street Journal,* January 25, 1993; David Stipp, "Yankee Atomic Spotlights Massive Costs Needed to Decommission Nuclear Plants," *Wall Street Journal,* June 2, 1992.

PHOTOVOLTAIC SALES GROWTH SLOWS

1. Paul D. Maycock, *Photovoltaic News,* February 1993.
2. Ibid.
3. Ibid.
4. Ibid.
5. William W.S. Charters, "Solar Energy: Current Status and Future Prospects," *Energy Policy,* October 1991.
6. Christopher Flavin and Nicholas Lenssen, *Beyond the Petroleum Age: Designing a Solar Economy,* Worldwatch Paper 100 (Washington, D.C.: Worldwatch Institute, December 1990).
7. Derek Lovejoy, "Electrification of Rural Areas by Solar PV," *Natural Resources Forum,* May 1992; Mark Hankins, *Solar Rural Electrification in the Developing World: Four Country Case Studies* (Washington, D.C.: Solar Electric Light Fund, 1993).
8. U.S. Department of Energy, "Introduction," presentations at the Photovoltaics: Investing in Development Conference, New Orleans, La., May 4-6, 1987.
9. Organisation for Economic Co-operation and Development (OECD), International Energy Agency (IEA), *Energy Policies of IEA Countries, Review 1991* (Paris: 1992).
10. Ibid.
11. Ibid.
12. OECD, IEA, *Energy Policies of IEA Countries* (Paris: various years).
13. Marty Rush, National Renewable Energy Laboratory, Golden, Colo., private communication, March 22, 1993; large-scale solar-electric power is available for 30–50¢ per kilowatt-hour, while small-scale costs slightly more.

GEOTHERMAL POWER GAINS

1. United Nations, *Energy Statistics Yearbook* (New York: various years).
2. Ronald DiPippo, "Geothermal Energy," *Energy Policy,* October 1991.
3. D.H. Freeston, "Direct Uses of Geothermal Energy in 1990," *Geothermal Resources Council Bulletin,* July/August 1990.
4. Renew America, *Sustainable Energy* (Washington, D.C.: 1989).
5. United Nations, *1990 Energy Statistics Yearbook* (New York: 1992).
6. Gerald W. Huttrer, "Geothermal Electric Power—A 1990 World Status Update," *Geothermal Resources Council Bulletin,* July/August 1990.
7. DiPippo, op. cit. note 2; Robin Bromby, "Geothermal Power to Supplant Hydro As Top Philippine Electric Choice," *The Solar Letter,* October 16, 1992.
8. Huttrer, op. cit. note 6.
9. Lian Nemenzo, "On a Dormant Volcano, Tribes Fight Power Project," *Subtext,* November 1992; "Mt. Apo Update," *Japan Environment Monitor,* June 30, 1992.
10. DiPippo, op. cit. note 2.
11. Edwin Karmiol, "Japan Awakening to Potential of Domestic Geothermal Energy," *The Solar Letter,* November 13, 1992.
12. Robert Corzine, "Purity in a Cold Climate," *Financial Times,* December 16, 1992.
13. Nancy Rader, *Power Surge: The Status and Near-Term Potential of Renewable Energy Technologies* (Washington, D.C.: Public Citizen, 1989), cited in Renew America, op. cit. note 4.
14. U.S. Department of Energy (DOE), Energy Information Administration, *Monthly Energy Review October 1992* (Washington: 1992).
15. DOE, "U.S. Geothermal Energy R&D Program Multiyear Plan, 1988-1992," Washington, D.C., October 1988, cited in Renew America, op. cit. note 4.
16. Organisation for Economic Co-operation and Development, *Renewable Sources of Energy* (Paris: 1987).

COAL USE GROWTH ENDS

1. British Petroleum (BP), *BP Statistical Review of World Energy* (London: 1992); United Nations, *1990 Energy Statistics Yearbook* (New York: 1992).
2. BP, op. cit. note 1.
3. United Nations, *Energy Statistics Yearbook* (New York: various years).
4. U.S. Department of Energy (DOE), Energy Information Administration, *Annual Energy Review 1991* (Washington, D.C.: 1992).
5. M.J. Chadwick and M. Hutton, *Acid Depositions in Europe: Environmental Effects, Control Strategies, and Policy Options* (Stockholm: Stockholm Environment Institute, 1991).
6. Worldwatch Institute estimate based on Tom Boden, Oak Ridge National Laboratory, Oak Ridge, Tenn., private communication and computer database, July 28, 1992.
7. International Energy Agency, *Energy Prices and Taxes, Third Quarter, 1992* (Paris: Organisation for Economic Co-operation and Development, 1992).
8. See, for example, Michael Heseltine, "Coal on His Christmas List," *Financial Times*, November 30, 1992.
9. Nicholas D. Kristof, "China Plans Big Layoffs of Coal Mine Workers," *New York Times*, December 29, 1992; "Coal Miners' Strike Spreads in Poland," *Journal of Commerce*, December 18, 1992; Stephen Engelberg, "Coal Miners in Poland Strike Over Wages and Job Threats," *New York Times*, December 18, 1992.
10. DOE, op. cit. note 4; jobs from U.S. Bureau of the Census, *Statistical Abstract of the United States 1991* (Washington, D.C.: 1991).
11. BP, op. cit. note 1.
12. P.T. Bangsberg, "China to Upgrade, Add Power Plants to Fuel Growth," *Journal of Commerce*, December 22, 1992; P.T. Bangsberg, "China Opens Second Stage of 'Energy Lifeline' Cola Project," *Journal of Commerce*, December 23, 1992.
13. BP, op. cit. note 1.

HYDROELECTRIC POWER GROWTH STEADY

1. British Petroleum (BP), *BP Statistical Review of World Energy* (London: 1992); United Nations, *1990 Energy Statistics Yearbook* (New York: 1992).
2. United Nations, *World Energy Supplies 1950–74* (New York: 1976); United Nations, *Energy Statistics Yearbook* (New York: various years).
3. United Nations, op. cit. note 1.
4. Eric M. Wilson, "Small-scale Hydroelectricity," *Energy Policy*, October 1991.
5. Geoffrey P. Sims, "Hydroelectric Energy," *Energy Policy*, October 1991.
6. BP, op. cit. note 1.
7. Ibid.
8. "Scandinavian Power Use Drops," *European Energy Review*, September 18, 1992.
9. Nancy Rader, *Power Surge: The Status and Near-Term Potential of Renewable Energy Technologies* (Washington, D.C.: Public Citizen, 1989), cited in Renew America, *Sustainable Energy* (Washington, D.C.: 1989).
10. U.S. Department of Energy, *Energy Security: A Report to the President of the United States* (Washington, D.C.: 1987), cited in Renew America, op. cit. note 9.
11. Renew America, op. cit. note 9.
12. Christopher Hocker, "The Miniboom In Pumped Storage," *Independent Energy*, March 1990.
13. Sims, op. cit. note 5.
14. "Battle to Build Dam Over Yangtze Is Struggle for the Heart of China," *Journal of Commerce*, December 23, 1992.
15. Clarence Maloney, "Environmental and Project Displacement of Population in India, Part I: Development and Deracination," *Field Staff Reports* (Sausalito, Calif.: Natural Heritage Institute, 1990-91).

CARBON EFFICIENCY DOWN SLIGHTLY

1. World Bank, Washington, D.C., unpublished printout, February 1992; gross world product from 1950 and 1955 from Herbert R. Block, *The Planetary Product in 1980: A Creative Pause?* (Washington, D.C.: U.S. Department of State, 1981); International Monetary Fund (IMF), *World Economic Outlook October 1992* (Washington, D.C.: 1992); Thomas A. Boden et al., *Trends '91: A Compendium of Data on Global Change* (Oak Ridge, Tenn.: Oak Ridge National Laboratory, 1991); British Petroleum (BP), *BP Statistical Review of World Energy* (London: various years).
2. For information on economic costs of carbon dioxide pollution and global warming, see William R. Cline, *Global Warming: The Economic Stakes* (Washington, D.C.: Institute for International Economics, 1992).
3. IMF, *World Economic Outlook May 1992* (Washington, D.C.: 1992).
4. Boden et al., op. cit. note 1; World Bank, *World Tables 1992* (Baltimore, Md.: Johns Hopkins University Press, 1992).
5. BP, op. cit. note 1; United Nations, *World Energy*

Supplies 1950–74 (New York: 1976); World Bank, Washington, D.C., private communication and print-out, August 24, 1992.

6. Edwin Moore and Enrique Crousillat, "Prospects for Gas-Fueled Combined-Cycle Power Generation," and Robert H. Williams and Eric D. Larson, "Expanding Roles for Gas Turbines in Power Generation," in Thomas B. Johansson et al., eds., *Electricity: Efficient End-Use and New Generation Technologies, and Their Planning Implications* (Lund, Sweden: Lund University Press, 1990).

7. Mark D. Levine et al., *Electricity End-Use Efficiency: Experience with Technologies, Markets, and Policies Throughout the World* (Berkeley, Calif.: Lawrence Berkeley Laboratory, 1992).

8. BP, op. cit. note 1; United Nations, op. cit. note 5; World Bank, op. cit. note 5.

9. Cline, op. cit. note 2.

10. U.N. Conference on Environment and Development Secretariat, "154 Signatures on Climate Convention in Rio," press release, Rio de Janeiro, June 14, 1992.

COMPACT FLUORESCENTS CATCHING ON

1. Evan Mills, Lawrence Berkeley Laboratory, Berkeley, Calif., private communication, February 3, 1993.

2. Ibid.

3. Worldwatch estimate, based on 800-megawatt generating capacity and 15-watt CFLs replacing 60-watt incandescents.

4. Mills, op. cit. note 1.

5. Worldwatch estimates, assuming a $15 price for CFLs and 75¢ for incandescents.

6. Mills, op. cit. note 1.

7. Michael Siminovitch, Lawrence Berkeley Laboratory, Berkeley, Calif., private communication, February 4, 1993.

8. Mark D. Levine et al., *Electricity End-Use Efficiency: Experience with Technologies, Markets, and Policies Throughout the World* (Berkeley, Calif.: Lawrence Berkeley Laboratory, 1992).

9. International Energy Agency (IEA), *Energy Prices and Taxes, Third Quarter, 1992* (Paris: Organisation for Economic Co-operation and Development (OECD), 1992); Worldwatch estimates of net present value of the payback from replacing a 60-watt incandescent bulb with a 15-watt CFL, using a 5-percent annual rate of return on five-year savings and a price of 75¢ for incandescent bulbs.

10. Worldwatch estimates based on IEA, *Electricity End-Use Efficiency* (Paris: OECD, 1989), and on U.S. Department of Energy, Energy Information Administration, *Annual Energy Review 1991* (Washington, D.C.: U.S. Government Printing Office, 1992).

11. Gilberto Jannuzzi, University of Campinas, Brazil, private communication, February 12, 1993; Peter Bleasby, Engineering Department, Osram/Sylvania Inc., Montgomery, N.Y., private communication, February 4, 1993.

CFC PRODUCTION FALLING

1. E.I. Du Pont de Nemours, Wilmington, Del., private communication, March 5, 1993.

2. Mario Molina and F. Sherwood Rowland, "Stratospheric Sink for Chlorofluoromethanes: Chlorine Atom Catalyzed Destruction of Ozone," *Nature*, June 28, 1974.

3. Joseph C. Farman et al., "Large Losses of Total Ozone in Antarctica Reveal Seasonal CLO_x/NO_x Interaction," *Nature*, May 16, 1985.

4. U.N. Environment Programme, "Montreal Protocol on Substances that Deplete the Ozone Layer," Nairobi, 1987.

5. United Nations' Synthesis of the Reports of the Ozone Scientific Assessment Panel, Environmental Effects Assessment Panel, and Technology and Economic Assessment Panel, prepared by the Assessment Chairs for the Parties to the Montreal Protocol, November 1991.

6. William K. Stevens, "Peril to Ozone Hastens a Ban on Chemicals," *New York Times*, November 26, 1992.

7. United Nations' Synthesis, op. cit. note 5.

8. Friends of the Earth International, "National Action Plans to Save the Ozone Layer: Countries' Restrictions on Ozone-Depleting Chemicals," London, undated.

9. World Meteorological Organization Global Ozone Research and Monitoring Project, "Scientific Assessment of Ozone Depletion 1991," Report No. 25, Geneva, 1991.

10. Ibid.

11. "Ozone Hole Over Antarctica Largest Ever, Satellite Shows," *Washington Post*, September 30, 1992.

12. United Nations' Synthesis, op. cit. note 5.

13. Ibid.

14. Friends of the Earth International, "At the Crossroads: The Multilateral Fund of the Montreal Protocol," London, November 1992.

15. "UN Conference Agrees to Accelerate Phase-out of Ozone Destroying Gases," *Journal of Commerce*, November 11, 1992.

GLOBAL TEMPERATURE DROPS

1. Helene Wilson, Columbia University and NASA Goddard Institute for Space Studies, New York, private communication, February 23, 1993.
2. Thomas R. Karl et al., "The Climate of 1992: Volcanic Clouds, El Nino, and Global Warming—An Overview," National Oceanic and Atmospheric Administration, press briefing, January 13, 1993.
3. Larry L. Stowe, "Monitoring the Volcanic Cloud of 1991/92," NOAA, press briefing, January 13, 1993; Richard A. Kerr, "Pinatubo Global Cooling on Target," *Science*, January 29, 1993.
4. Data for 1959–90 from Charles O. Keeling and data for 1991–92 from Timothy Whorf, Scripps Institute of Oceanography, La Jolla, Calif., private communications, February 26, 1993.
5. Intergovernmental Panel on Climate Change (IPCC), *Climate Change: The IPCC Scientific Assessment 1991* (Cambridge, U.K.: World Meteorological Organization/United Nations Environment Programme, 1991).
6. U.S. Department of Agriculture, *World Grain Situation and Outlook,* Washington, D.C., various issues.
7. International Monetary Fund, *International Financial Statistics,* various issues.
8. IPCC, op. cit. note 5.

GLOBAL ECONOMY EXPANDS SLOWLY

1. International Monetary Fund (IMF), *World Economic Outlook: Interim Assessment* (Washington, D.C.: January 1993).
2. Ibid.
3. Ibid.
4. Steven Greenhouse, "Gloomy Prospects Seen for Growth Worldwide in '93," *New York Times,* December 21, 1992.
5. IMF, op. cit. note 1.
6. "China Says Growth at 12 Percent," *New York Times,* December 31, 1992.
7. IMF, op. cit. note 1.
8. Stephen Engelberg, "Twenty-one Months of 'Shock Therapy' Resuscitates Polish Economy," *New York Times,* December 17, 1992.
9. "China Forecasts Big Increase in Timber Exports This Year," *Journal of Commerce,* February 17, 1993; B. Bowonder et al., *Deforestation and Fuelwood Use in Urban Centres* (Hyderabad, India: Centre for Energy, Environment, and Technology and National

Remote Sensing Agency, 1985); "New Deforestation Rate Figures Announced," *Tropical Forest Programme* (IUCN Newsletter), August 1990.
10. Harold Dregne et al., "A New Assessment of the World's Status of Desertification," *Desertification Control Bulletin* (U.N. Environment Programme), No. 20, 1991.
11. World Resources Institute, *World Resources 1988–89* (New York: Basic Books, 1988).
12. Sandra Postel, *Last Oasis: Facing Water Scarcity* (New York: W.W. Norton and Company, 1992).

TRADE CONTINUES STEEP RISE

1. International Monetary Fund, Washington, D.C., unpublished data base; World Bank, Washington, D.C., unpublished data base.
2. General Agreement on Tariffs and Trade Secretariat, "GATT: What It Is, What It Does," Geneva, 1991.
3. Herman Daly and Robert Goodland, "An Ecological-Economic Assessment of Deregulation of International Commerce Under GATT" (draft), World Bank, Washington, D.C., undated.
4. World Resources Institute, *World Resources 1992–93* (New York: Oxford University Press, 1992).
5. U.N. Conference on Trade and Development, *Trade and Development Report 1991* (Geneva: 1991).
6. Christopher Stevens, Overseas Development Institute, London, private communication, March 1992.
7. Robin Broad and John Cavanagh, "No More NICs," *Foreign Policy,* Fall 1988.
8. Hilary F. French, *Costly Tradeoffs: Reconciling Trade and the Environment,* Worldwatch Paper 113 (Washington, D.C.: Worldwatch Institute, March 1993).

STEEL PRODUCTION FALLS

1. International Iron and Steel Institute, *Steel Statistical Yearbook 1992* (Brussels: 1992).
2. Ibid.
3. "European Steel Gloom Deepens," *Wall Street Journal,* March 26, 1993.
4. G.W. Houck, U.S. Bureau of Mines, private communication, March 15, 1993.
5. Ibid.; International Iron and Steel Institute, *Steel Statistical Yearbook 1991* (Brussels: 1991).
6. Dwight K. French, U.S. Department of Energy (DOE), Office of Energy Markets and End Use, Washington, D.C., private communication, November 24, 1992; DOE, Energy Information Administration (EIA), *Manufacturing Energy Consumption Sur-*

vey: Consumption of Energy 1988 (Washington, D.C.: U.S. Government Printing Office, 1988).

7. DOE, EIA, Annual Energy Review 1991 (Washington, D.C.: U.S. Government Printing Office, 1992).

8. Louis Uchitelle, "On the Path to an Open Economy, A Decrepit Steel Plant in the Urals," New York Times, July 2, 1992; Daniel Sneider, "The Soviet Ecocidal Legacy," Christian Science Monitor, June 11, 1992.

9. Uchitelle, op. cit. note 8; Sneider, op. cit. note 8.

10. International Iron and Steel Institute, op. cit. note 1.

11. Donald F. Barnett and Robert W. Crandall, Up From The Ashes: The Rise of the Steel Minimill in the United States (Washington, D.C.: Brookings Institution, 1986).

12. Eric D. Larson, Marc H. Ross, and Robert H. Williams, "Beyond the Era of Materials," Scientific American, June 1986.

13. International Iron and Steel Institute, op. cit. note 1.

PAPER PRODUCTION CONTINUES GROWTH

1. Annual production data for 1980-90 from United Nations Statistical Division, 1988/89 Statistical Yearbook (New York: 1992); 1991 from Pulp and Paper International, July 1991; 1992 estimate based on data from American Paper Institute, private communication, January 1993, and from Pulp and Paper International, January 1993.

2. Claudia G. Thompson, Recycled Papers: The Essential Guide (Cambridge, Mass: The MIT Press, 1992); growth rates based on production data from United Nations, op. cit. note 1, and from Pulp and Paper International, January 1993.

3. U.S. figure from Thompson, op. cit. note 2; world figure from Pulp and Paper International, July 1991.

4. Vivian Pharis, "World Pulp Trends Bode Ill For Industry, Well For Its Forests," Wilderness Alberta, June 1992.

5. Pulp and Paper International, January 1993.

6. Ibid.

7. "Indonesia Leads the Drive for Expansion," Financial Times, December 14, 1992.

8. Number of trees is based on an estimate of 17 trees per ton of paper produced, from Conservatree, Inc., San Francisco, 1992.

9. Forest loss based on Sandra Postel and John C. Ryan, "Reforming Forestry," in Lester R. Brown et al., State of the World 1991 (New York: W.W. Norton and Company, 1991).

10. Pharis, op. cit. note 4.

11. The Japanese paper, called Lotus Gloss, is made by Honshu Paper Company; its composition was reported by Hayden-Cary & King (paper broker), Darien, Conn., private communication, July 1992; China recycling figure from Pharis, op. cit. note 4.

12. Jackie Cox, "Lyons Falls Is First in U.S. To Make Chlorine-Free Printing Paper," American Papermaker, January 1992.

13. American Paper Institute, "Year to Year Percentage Change in Pulping and Bleaching Chemicals Used by U.S. Pulp and Paper Industry," 1992, extrapolated from a 94-percent survey sample of U.S. bleached pulp capacity.

WORLD SPENDING ON ADS SKYROCKETS

1. Rate of growth adjusted for inflation; 1950 and 1960 from Robert J. Coen, International Herald Tribune, October 10, 1984, cited in Frederick Clairmonte and John Cavanagh, Merchants of Drink (Penang, Malaysia: Third World Network, 1988); more recent years from Tracy Poltie, International Advertising Association, New York, private communications, August 29, 1990, and January 15, 1992.

2. Lester R. Brown, Christopher Flavin, and Hal Kane, Vital Signs 1992 (New York: W.W. Norton and Company, 1992).

3. Monetary figures expressed in constant 1989 dollars; 1950 from Coen, op. cit. note 1; 1990 from Poltie, op. cit. note 1; Indian gross national product from World Bank, World Development Report 1991 (New York: Oxford University Press, 1991); health and education expenditures from Ruth Leger Sivard, World Military and Social Expenditures 1990–91 (Washington, D.C.: World Priorities, 1991).

4. Per capita figures derived from Coen, op. cit. note 1, from Poltie, op. cit. note 1, and from Center for International Research, U.S. Bureau of the Census, Washington, D.C., private communication, March 26, 1993.

5. For a full discussion of these points, see Alan Thein Durning, How Much Is Enough? (New York: W.W. Norton and Company, 1992).

6. Coen, op. cit. note 1; Poltie, op. cit. note 1.

7. Poltie, op. cit. note 1.

8. U.S. 1950–89 per capita from U.S. Department of Commerce, Historical Statistics of the United States, Colonial Times to 1970, Bicentennial Edition, Part 2 (Washington, D.C.: 1975), and from U.S. Department of Commerce, Bureau of the Census, Statistical Abstract of the United States: 1990 (Washington, D.C.: U.S. Government Printing Office, 1990); U.S. 1990 per capita from Crain Communications,

Inc., Chicago, Ill., private communication, January 17, 1992; 1991 from *Advertising Age,* May 4, 1992.

9. Poltie, op. cit. note 1; Population Reference Bureau (PRB), *World Population Data Sheet 1990* (Washington, D.C.: 1990).

10. Poltie, op. cit. note 1; PRB, op. cit. note 9.

11. Quoted in Guy de Jonquieres, "Home-grown Produce on the Multinationals' Shopping List," *Financial Times,* August 8, 1991.

12. Poltie, op. cit. note 1; PRB, op. cit. note 9.

13. Korea from "Asia's Network Boom," *Asiaweek,* July 6, 1990; Prakash Chandra, "India: Middle-Class Spending," *Third World Week* (Institute for Current World Affairs, Hanover, N.H.), March 2, 1990; India per capita from Poltie, op. cit. note 1, and from PRB, op. cit. note 9.

14. Poltie, op. cit. note 1; PRB, op. cit. note 9.

15. Quoted in *Fortune,* March 26, 1990.

16. Durning, op. cit. note 5.

THIRD WORLD DEBT RISING SLOWLY

1. International Monetary Fund, *World Economic Outlook: Interim Assessment* (Washington, D.C.: January 1993).

2. World Bank, *World Debt Tables 1991–92* (Washington, D.C.: 1992).

3. Calculation by Nick Lenssen, Worldwatch Institute, based on Mark D. Levine et al., *Energy Efficiency, Developing Nations, and Eastern Europe,* A Report to the U.S. Working Group on Global Energy Efficiency (Washington, D.C.: International Institute for Energy Conservation, 1991).

4. Lawrence H. Summers, *Investing in All the People* (Washington, D.C.: World Bank, 1992), cited in the Institute for International Economics, *International Economic Insights* (Washington, D.C.: 1992).

5. See, for example, Catherine Gwin et al., *The International Monetary Fund in a Multipolar World: Pulling Together* (New Brunswick, N.J.: Transaction Books for Overseas Development Council, 1989), and Dharam Ghai, ed., *The IMF And The South: The Social Impact of Crisis and Adjustment* (London: Zed Books, 1991).

6. Wilfrido Cruz and Robert Repetto, *The Environmental Effects of Stabilization and Structural Adjustment Programs: The Philippines Case* (Washington, D.C.: World Resources Institute, 1992); David Reed, ed., *Structural Adjustment and the Environment* (Boulder, Colo.: Westview Press, 1992).

7. Cruz and Repetto, op. cit. note 6.

BICYCLE PRODUCTION RESUMES CLIMB

1. *Interbike Directory 1993* (Costa Mesa, Calif.: Primedia, Inc., 1993).

2. Bicycles from United Nations, Statistical Office, *The Growth of World Industry, Vol. II: Commodity Production Data, 1958–1967* (New York: 1970); cars from Motor Vehicle Manufacturers Association (MVMA), *World Motor Vehicle Data,* 1992 ed. (Detroit, Mich.: 1992).

3. United Nations, op. cit. note 2; MVMA, op. cit. note 2.

4. Robert Boivin and Jean-Francois Pronovost, eds., *The Bicycle: Global Perspectives,* papers presented at the Conference Velo Mondiale, Montreal, September 13–17, 1992 (Montreal: Velo Quebec, 1992).

5. Author's estimate based on Boivin and Pronovost, op. cit. note 4, and on data base on purchasing power developed for Alan Thein Durning, *How Much Is Enough?* (New York: W.W. Norton and Company, 1992).

6. Bicycle Institute of America (BIA), *Bicycling Reference Book,* 1992–1993 ed. (Washington, D.C.: 1992).

7. Number of bicycles in China from *Interbike Directory 1993,* op. cit. note 1; number of cars from MVMA, op. cit. note 2.

8. Government of China, *China Statistics Yearbook* (Beijing: 1992).

9. *Interbike Directory 1993,* op. cit. note 1; automobile production from MVMA, Detroit, Mich., private communication, March 24, 1992, and from Motor Vehicle Manufacturers Association of Italy (ANFIA), "Le Potenze Mondiali dell'Auto," Torino, Italy, 1992.

10. *Interbike Directory 1993,* op. cit. note 1.

11. Ibid.; population data from Population Reference Bureau, *1992 World Population Data Sheet* (Washington, D.C.: 1992).

12. Author's estimate based on a 1991 figure of 3.5 million from BIA, op. cit. note 6, and on Suzanne Alexander, "Riding a Bike to Work Gains in Popularity," *Wall Street Journal,* December 26, 1991.

AUTO PRODUCTION FLAT

1. Production in 1950-90 from Motor Vehicle Manufacturers Association (MVMA), *Facts & Figures '92* and *World Motor Vehicle Data,* 1991 ed. (Detroit, Mich.: 1991); 1991 production from Kevin Done, "World Car Industry: The Engine Overheats," *Financial Times,* October 10, 1992; 1992 production in Japan

from Japan Automobile Manufacturers Association, personal communication, March 26, 1993; 1992 production in the United States, Canada, Korea, Brazil, Mexico, and Europe from *Automotive News,* various issues, January and February 1993.

2. Sales from *Automotive News,* February 8, 1993.
3. "Auto Industry is Hit By a Global Shakeout; Even Japanese Suffer," *Wall Street Journal,* December 29, 1992; Done, op. cit. note 1.
4. GM closings from Kevin Done, "A New Car Industry Set to Rise in the East," *Financial Times,* September 24, 1992; Nissan cuts from Kevin Done, "Japan's Car Industry at Crossroads," *Financial Times,* October 7, 1992; Isuzu discontinuation from Andrew Pollack, "Isuzu to Stop Manufacturing Passenger Cars," *New York Times,* October 2, 1992.
5. Done, "Japan's Car Industry," op. cit. note 4.
6. U.S. sales from David R. Francis, "Big 3 Hope U.S. Leads World Out of Slump," *Christian Science Monitor,* December 12, 1992; European sales from Kevin Done, "European Car Sales Surprise the Industry," *Financial Times,* January 1, 1993; Japanese from Clayton Jones, "Japan's First Auto Crisis," *Christian Science Monitor,* December 2, 1992.
7. John Burton, "Seven May Not Be a Lucky Number," *Financial Times,* October 20, 1992.
8. Warren Brown and Frank Swoboda, "GM Announces Series of Steps to Cut Costs," *Washington Post,* October 24, 1992.
9. Done, "A New Car Industry," op. cit. note 4.
10. Ibid.
11. Kevin Done, "Car Production Goes From 0 to 130,-000 in 14 Weeks," *Financial Times,* September 23, 1992.
12. Laurent Belsie, "Rough Road for the World Auto Industry," *Christian Science Monitor,* December 2, 1992.
13. James J. MacKenzie, Roger C. Dower and Donald D.T. Chen, *The Going Rate: What it Really Costs to Drive* (Washington, D.C.: World Resources Institute, 1992); Ed Ayres, "Breaking Away," *World Watch,* January/February 1993.
14. Stephen Joseph, "The Climate is Changing," *Financial Times,* October 20, 1992.

AIR TRAVEL GROWTH RESUMES

1. International Civil Aviation Organization (ICAO), Montreal, various tables and reports between the fifties and 1992.
2. Ibid.
3. Ibid.

4. Worldwatch calculations based on Stacy Davis and Melissa Morris, *Transportation Energy Data Book: Edition 12* (Oak Ridge, Tenn: Oak Ridge National Laboratory, 1992).
5. Mary C. Holcomb et al., *Transportation Energy Data Book: Edition 9* (Oak Ridge, Tenn.: Oak Ridge National Laboratory, 1987).
6. Daniel B. Wood, "New 777 Loaded With Innovations," *Christian Science Monitor,* December 21, 1990.
7. United Nations, *1990 Energy Statistics Yearbook* (New York: 1992).
8. Robert A. Egli, "Climate: Air-Traffic Emissions," *Environment,* November 1991.
9. Ibid.
10. Ibid.
11. Ibid.; William K. Stevens, "Global Warming Threat Found in Aircraft Fumes," *New York Times,* January 7, 1992.
12. Robert A. Egli, "Nitrogen Oxide Emissions from Air Traffic," *Technologie,* November 1990.
13. Egli, op. cit. note 8; Mark Barrett, "Aircraft Pollution, Environmental Impacts and Future Solutions," World Wide Fund For Nature-UK/Earth Resources Research, London, August 1991.

POPULATION GROWTH SETS ANOTHER RECORD

1. Center for International Research, U.S. Bureau of the Census, Washington, D.C., private communication, May 11, 1993.
2. Population Reference Bureau (PRB), *1993 World Population Data Sheet* (Washington, D.C.: 1993).
3. World Bank, *World Tables 1991* (Washington, D.C.: 1991); World Bank, *World Development Report 1992* (New York: Oxford University Press, 1992).
4. Statement of Ji Chaozhu, Under-Secretary General, Department of Economic and Social Development, press conference, United Nations, New York, July 10, 1992.
5. PRB, op. cit. note 2.
6. United Nations, Statistical Division, *Population and Vital Statistics Report,* New York, January 1993.
7. PRB, op. cit. note 2.
8. United Nations, op. cit. note 6.
9. United Nations, Population Divison, "Urban Agglomerations 1992," New York, 1992.
10. PRB, op. cit. note 2.
11. PRB, *1991 World Population Data Sheet* (Washington, D.C.: 1991).
12. PRB, op. cit. note 2.
13. PRB, op, cit. note 11.

14. PRB, op. cit. note 2.
15. For a discussion of the influences of these two pressures, see Alan Thein Durning, *How Much Is Enough?* (New York: W.W. Norton and Company, 1992).
16. This figure is the total for world population under the medium variant projections; United Nations, *World Population Prospects: The 1992 Revision* (New York: forthcoming).
17. Shiro Horiuchi, "Stagnation in the Decline of the World Population Growth Rate During the 1980s," *Science*, August 7, 1992.

CHILD MORTALITY CONTINUES TO FALL

1. United Nations, Department of International Economic and Social Affairs, *Mortality of Children Under Age 5: World Estimates and Projections, 1950–2025* (New York: 1988).
2. James P. Grant, "250,000 Children Die Each Week," *CEO International Strategies*, October/November 1992.
3. W. Henry Mosley and Peter Cowley, *The Challenge of World Health* (Washington, D.C.: Population Reference Bureau, December 1991).
4. Ibid.
5. United Nations, op. cit. note 1.
6. UNICEF, *State of the World's Children 1992* (New York: Oxford University Press, 1992).
7. Ibid.
8. Alan D. Lopez, "Causes of Death: An Assessment of Global Patterns of Mortality Around 1950," *World Health Statistical Quarterly*, Vol. 43, 1990, pp. 91–104, cited in Mosley and Cowley, op. cit. note 3.
9. UNICEF, op. cit. note 6.
10. Shea O. Rutstein, "Levels, Trends and Differentials in Infant and Child Mortality in the Less Developed Countries," presented at the seminar on Child Survival Interventions: Effectiveness and Efficiency at The Johns Hopkins University School of Hygiene and Public Health, Baltimore, Md., 20–22 June, 1991, cited in Mosley and Cowley, op. cit. note 3.

CIGARETTE SMOKING DROPS AGAIN

1. Historical data from Dan Stevens, U.S. Department of Agriculture (USDA), Foreign Agricultural Service (FAS), unpublished printout, November 7, 1991; data for 1950–59 simple arithmetic extrapolations based on U.S. data; revisions of recent numbers and updates from USDA, FAS, private communication, March 15, 1993.

2. U.S. rate from USDA, Economic Research Service, unpublished printout, private communication, March 24, 1993.
3. Worldwatch calculations with data from USDA, *World Tobacco Situation*, August 1992.
4. Ibid.
5. Grace M. Kang, "Smoking Issue Is Heating Up Custody Suits," *Wall Street Journal*, August 17, 1992.
6. Paul Raeburn, "EPA Report Calls Cigarette Smoke 'Substantial' Risk for Nonsmokers," *Washington Post*, January 8, 1993.
7. Sandy Rovner, "Oncologists Ask Large Cigarette Tax Increase," *Washington Post*, December 20, 1992.
8. Alice Rawsthorn, "France's Smoking Habit Given a Kick," *Financial Times*, June 1, 1992.
9. Steven Erlanger, "R.J. Reynolds in Russia: Can Josef Camel Be Far Behind?" *New York Times*, August 1, 1992.
10. Philip Rawstorne, "BAT Poised to Light Up New Market," *Financial Times*, November 4, 1992.
11. Roger Cohen, "Philip Morris to Buy Control of Czech Cigarette Maker," *New York Times*, May 21, 1992.
12. Jonathan Kaufman, "US Tobacco Firms Find Big Market in E. Europe," *Journal of Commerce*, May 29, 1992.
13. "Asian Countries Say No to US Cancer Sticks," *Down to Earth*, June 30, 1992; James L. Tyson, "Chinese Light, and Fight, Tobacco," *Christian Science Monitor*, June 23, 1992.
14. USDA, op. cit. note 2; USDA, *Tobacco Situation and Outlook Yearbook* (Washington, D.C.: 1992).
15. USDA, "Commodity Spotlight," *Agricultural Outlook*, May 1992.
16. "Smoking: Good News and Bad" (editorial), *Washington Post*, May 24, 1992.
17. Ibid.

REFUGEES REACH ALL-TIME RECORD

1. U.N. High Commision on Refugees (UNHCR), Washington, D.C. office, private communication, March 19, 1993.
2. United Nations Population Fund, *The State of World Population 1992* (New York: 1992).
3. UNHCR, op cit. note 1.
4. U.S. Committee for Refugees, *World Refugee Survey 1992* (Washington, D.C.: 1992).
5. Ibid.
6. Clarence Maloney, "Environmental and Project Displacement of Population in India, Part I: Development and Deracination," *Field Staff Reports*

(Sausalito, Calif.: Natural Heritage Institute, 1990–91).

WATER SCARCITY SPREADING

1. United Nations, Department of International Economic and Social Affairs, *World Population Prospects 1990* (New York: 1991); World Resources Institute (WRI), *World Resources 1992–93* (New York: Oxford University Press, 1992).
2. Malin Falkenmark, "The Massive Water Scarcity Now Threatening Africa—Why Isn't it Being Addressed?" *Ambio*, Vol. 18, No. 2, 1989.
3. The four additional countries are Malawi, Morocco, South Africa, and Sudan.
4. World Bank, *World Development Report 1992* (New York: Oxford University Press, 1992).
5. John B. Weeks, "High Plains Regional Aquifer-System Study," in Ren Jen Sun, ed., *Regional Aquifer-System Analysis Program of the U.S. Geological Survey: Summary of Projects, 1978–84* (Washington, D.C.: U.S. Government Printing Office, 1986).
6. Depletion figure from tables supplied by the High Plains Underground Water Conservation District No. 1, Lubbock, Tex., dated May 3, 1991; Texas water use, preliminary estimates, from Wayne Solley, Water Use Information, U.S. Geological Survey, Reston, Va., private communication, April 27, 1992, with final estimates in *Estimated Use of Water in the United States in 1990* (Washington, D.C.: U.S. Government Printing Office, 1993).
7. Texas Water Development Board (TWDB), *Surveys of Irrigation in Texas—1958, 1964, 1969, 1974, 1979, 1984, and 1989* (Austin, Tex.: 1991); Comer Tuck, TWDB, Austin, Tex., private communication, November 26, 1991.
8. Population Reference Bureau, *1992 Population Data Sheet* (Washington, D.C.: 1992); WRI, op. cit. note 1.
9. James E. Nickum, "Beijing's Rural Water Use," prepared for East-West Center North China Project, Honolulu, Hawaii, March 1987; The Chinese Research Team for Water Resources Policy and Management in Beijing-Tianjin Region of China, *Report on Water Resources Policy and Management for the Beijing-Tianjin Region of China* (Beijing: Sino-US Cooperative Research Project on Water Resources Policy and Management, 1987); "Water Rules Tightened; Fines Levied," *China Daily*, May 18, 1989; North China Plain grain output from Frederick W. Crook, *Agricultural Statistics of the People's Republic of China, 1949–86* (Washington, D.C.: Economic Research Service, U.S. Department of Agriculture, 1988).

10. Li Hong, "Beijing Set to Tackle Water Thirst," *China Daily*, October 17, 1989.
11. "Northern, Coastal Area Cities Face Water Shortages," *China Daily*, August 29, 1991, as reprinted in *JPRS Report: Environmental Issues*, October 11, 1991.

AIR POLLUTION DAMAGING FORESTS

1. U.N. Economic Commission for Europe (ECE), Executive Body for the Convention on Long-range Transboundary Air Pollution, "Forest Condition in Europe: The 1992 Report," Geneva, September 14, 1992; "Forest Damage in Europe: What Surveying Shows," *Acid News* (Swedish and Norwegian NGO Secretariats on Acid Rain), December 1992.
2. M.J. Chadwick and M. Hutton, *Acid Depositions in Europe: Environmental Effects, Control Strategies, and Policy Options* (Stockholm: Stockholm Environment Institute, 1991); E.D. Schulze, "Air Pollution and Forest Decline in a Spruce *(Picea abies)* Forest," *Science*, May 19, 1989.
3. Harald Sverdrup et al., "Critical Loads for Forest Soils in the Nordic Countries," *Ambio*, August 1992.
4. ECE, op. cit. note 1; since most trees in the advanced stages of decline are removed from the forest, more have been affected than the survey results indicate.
5. "The Price of Pollution," *Options* (International Institute for Applied Systems Analysis), September 1990.
6. The $35-billion figure includes the value of the timber lost, the decline in value added in the basic processing of wood into products, and the loss of environmental and social benefits (such as protection of soil and water, sequestration of carbon, tourism, and recreation); Sten Nilsson, "Sustainability of European Forest Resources—A Case Study," *Ecological Economics*, forthcoming (revised for submission September 30, 1992); gross national product comparison based on International Monetary Fund, *International Financial Statistics*, March 1993.
7. Sten Nilsson et al., *Future Forest Resources of Western and Eastern Europe* (Carnforth, U.K.: Parthenon Publishing Group, 1992).
8. Sten Nilsson et al., *The Forest Resources of the Former European USSR* (Carnforth, U.K.: Parthenon Publishing Group, 1992).
9. Sverdrup et al., op. cit. note 3.
10. Between 1980 and 1993, the National Acid Precipitation Assessment Program (NAPAP) spent $635 million, according to April Maupin, Office of the Director, NAPAP, Washington, D.C., private commun-

ication, March 3, 1993; NAPAP, *1990 Integrated Assessment Report* (Washington, D.C.: 1991).

11. John Flynn, "How Congress Was Duped About Acid Rain's Effects," *Amicus Journal,* Winter 1991.

12. Ibid.

13. Ibid.

14. NAPAP, op. cit. note 10.

15. Ibid.

16. Chen Chuying et al., "Effects of Acid Rain on Forest Ecosystem in Southwestern China," *Journal of Environmental Sciences* (China), Vol. 3, 1991; "Strategy Set to Control Acid Rain," *China Environmental News,* January 1991.

17. William Chandler et al., "Energy for the Soviet Union, Eastern Europe and China," *Scientific American,* September 1990; damage estimate from "Acute Pollution," *China Daily,* February 22, 1993.

18. Increase in coal combustion from Zhou Dadi, Associate Director, Energy Research Institute, State Planning Commission of China, presentation given at the U.S.-China Conference on Energy, Environment, and Market Mechanisms, Washington, D.C., February 13, 1993; Henning Rodhe et al., "Acidification in Southeast Asia—Prospects for the Coming Decades," *Ambio,* April 1992.

19. Sten Nilsson and Ola Sallnäs, "Air Pollution and Forests: Policy Implications Based on Simulation Models," *Unasylva 163,* Vol. 41, No. 4, 1990.

20. Sten Nilsson, ed., *European Forest Decline: The Effects of Air Pollutants and Suggested Remedial Policies* (Stockholm, Sweden: International Institute for Applied Systems Analysis, Royal Swedish Academy of Agriculture and Forestry, and InterAction Council, 1991).

21. Fred Pearce, "Britain Faces High Bill to Cut Acid Rain," *New Scientist,* March 13, 1993.

22. Nilsson, op. cit. note 20.

23. Curtis Moore, "A Path Toward Zero Air Pollution: The Role of Today's Technologies," presented at the State and Territorial Air Pollution Program Administrators and the Association of Local Air Pollution Control Officials (STAPPA/ALAPCO) Workshop on Innovative Air Pollution Control Technologies, New Orleans, La., October 1989; Christopher Flavin and Nicholas Lenssen, *Beyond the Petroleum Age: Designing a Solar Economy,* Worldwatch Paper 100 (Washington, D.C.: Worldwatch Institute, December 1990).

MANY MARINE MAMMAL POPULATIONS DECLINING

1. John C. Ryan, *Life Support: Conserving Biological Diversity,* Worldwatch Paper 108 (Washington, D.C.: Worldwatch Institute, April 1992).

2. Dolphins from National Oceanic and Atmospheric Administration (NOAA), *Our Living Oceans: The First Annual Report on the Status of U.S. Living Marine Resources* (Washington, D.C.: 1991); John Harwood and Peter Reijnders, "Seals, Sense, and Sensibility," *New Scientist,* October 15, 1988.

3. Whale beachings from "Lost Angels: The Great Australian Whale Rescue," Storyteller Productions, Arts and Entertainment Network, January 28, 1993.

4. International Whaling Commission, Cambridge, U.K., private communication, September 1992; Ron Nowack, Office of Scientific Authority, U.S. Fish and Wildlife Service, Arlington, Va., private communication, January 1993.

5. NOAA, Office of Protected Resources, *Marine Mammal Protection Act of 1972, Annual Report 1988–89* (Washington, D.C.: U.S. Department of Commerce, 1992); Ron Nowack, *Walker's Mammals of the World* (Baltimore, Md.: Johns Hopkins University Press, 1991).

6. Kenneth S. Norris, "Dolphins in Crisis," *National Geographic,* September 1992.

7. Ibid.; NOAA, op. cit. note 2.

8. Norris, op. cit. note 6.

9. Nowack, op. cit. note 4.

10. NOAA, op. cit. note 2.

11. "Namibian Seals Face Extinction," *New African,* March 1990.

12. Animal Welfare Institute, *The Endangered Species Handbook* (Washington, D.C.: 1983).

13. NOAA, op. cit. note 2.

14. Harwood and Reijnders, op. cit. note 2.

15. NOAA, op. cit. note 2.

16. "Analysis of Propeller Wounds on Manatees in Florida," *Journal of Wildlife Management,* 46 (2), cited in Victoria Brook Van Meter, *The West Indian Manatee in Florida* (Florida Light & Power Company, 1989).

17. David Macdonald, ed., *The Encyclopedia of Mammals* (New York: Facts on File, 1984).

18. Nowack, op. cit. note 4.

19. International Union for Conservation of Nature and Natural Resources, World Wildlife Fund, and U.N. Environment Programme, *World Conservation Strategy* (Gland, Switzerland: 1980); Boyce Thorne-Miller and John Catena, *The Living Ocean: Understanding and Protecting Marine Biodiversity* (Washington, D.C.: Friends of the Earth, 1991); Norris, op. cit. note 6.

20. Alexander MacLeod, "World Whaling Body Shaken by Attempts to Resume the Hunt," *Christian Science Monitor,* July 6, 1992.

21. Marnie Stetson, "Saving Nature's Sunscreen," *World Watch,* March/April 1992.

WHEAT/OIL EXCHANGE RATE DROPS

1. International Monetary Fund, *International Statistics,* various years.
2. "Oversupply in Crude Oil Markets May Drag Down Prices Worldwide," *Journal of Commerce,* March 24, 1993.
3. U.S. Department of Agriculture, *World Grain Situation and Outlook,* Washington, D.C., February 1993.
4. International Monetary Fund, *International Financial Statistics,* January 1993.
5. Christopher Flavin, "Natural Gas Production Climbs," in Lester R. Brown, Christopher Flavin, and Hal Kane, *Vital Signs 1992* (New York: W.W. Norton and Company, 1992).
6. Author's personal observations.
7. Thomas C. Hayes, "Industry Guages Costs of Clinton Energy Tax," *New York Times,* February 19, 1993.
8. Timothy Noah, "Energy Tax Strives to Be Fair But Some Will Feel Picked On," *Wall Street Journal,* February 19, 1993.
9. Robert D. Hershey, Jr., "Indirect Effects of the Energy Tax," *New York Times,* February 20, 1993.
10. "Losses and Gains in Energy Bill," *Power Line,* November/December 1992.
11. Daniel Yergin, *The Prize: The Epic Quest for Oil, Money and Power* (New York: Simon and Schuster, 1991).

CIGARETTE TAXES ON THE RISE

1. "2 Studies Find Smoking Increases Cataract Risk," *Washington Post,* August 26, 1992.
2. "Mothers' Smoking Is Linked to Child," *New York Times,* September 8, 1992.
3. Timothy Noah, "EPA Declares 'Passive' Smoke a Human Carcinogen," *Wall Street Journal,* January 6, 1993.
4. Non-Smokers' Rights Association (NSRA) of Canada and the Council for a Tobacco-Free Ontario, "Health-Oriented Policy Options on Tobacco Tax in the 1992 Ontario Budget: A Submission to the Treasurer of Ontario," Ottawa, January 1992.
5. Kevin Sack, "21 Cent Tax Rise For Cigarettes Is Considered," *New York Times,* January 15, 1993.
6. Non-Smokers' Rights Association of Canada, Ottawa, private communication, March 15, 1993 (of table of January 4, 1993).
7. Ibid.

8. William V. George, U.S. Department of Agriculture, Foreign Agricultural Service, "Import Requirements and Restrictions for Tobacco and Tobacco Products In Foreign Markets" (draft of June 1992), Washington, D.C., unpublished.
9. U.S. Surgeon General, Pan American Health Organization (PAHO), and U.S. Centers for Disease Control (CDC), *Smoking and Health in the Americas* (Atlanta, Ga.: U.S. Department of Health and Human Services et al., 1992).
10. Ibid.
11. David Sweanor, NSRA of Canada, "The Role of Excise Taxes in Preventing Tobacco Use Among Young People," prepared for plenary address of Eighth World Conference on Tobacco or Health, Buenos Aires, April 1, 1992; NSRA of Canada, "Annual Per Capita Consumption of Cigarettes and Real Price of Tobacco (per 20 cigarettes), Canada, 1950–92," Ottawa, private communication, March 15, 1993.
12. Sweanor, op. cit. note 11.
13. U.S. Congress, Office of Technology Assessment (OTA), "Smoking-Related Deaths and Financial Costs" (draft), Washington, D.C., September 1985 (although this study is widely cited in the literature on this subject, it was never formally released by OTA).
14. Jimmy Carter, "To Save Lives, Raise Funds and Cut the Deficit: Tax Tobacco" (letter), *New York Times,* February 21, 1993.
15. All disease statistics from U.S. Surgeon General, PAHO, and CDC, op. cit. note 9.
16. Richard Peto et al., "Mortality from Tobacco in Developed Countries: Indirect Estimation from National Vital Statistics," *Lancet,* May 23, 1992.

U.S. SEAFOOD PRICES HAVE CLIMBED

1. U.S. Department of Labor, Bureau of Labor Statistics, Consumer Price Index (unpublished printout), October 2, 1992.
2. Ibid.; U.S. Department of Agriculture (USDA), Economic Research Service (ERS), "Red Meat, Poultry, and Fish (Boneless, Trimmed Equivalent): Per Capita Consumption, 1967–89," Washington, D.C., private communication, January 15, 1991.
3. See, for example, Lawrence Ingrassia, "Overfishing Threatens to Wipe Out Species and Crush Industry," *Wall Street Journal,* July 16, 1991.
4. U.N. Food and Agriculture Organization (FAO), Rome, private communication, March 23, 1993; meat from FAO, *FAO Production Yearbook* (Rome: various years), and from USDA, *World Agricultural Production,* August and September 1991.

5. FAO, *The State of Food and Agriculture 1989* (Rome: 1989).
6. David Blackwell, "EC Fish Deficit Widens as Demand Increases," *Financial Times*, September 3, 1992.
7. FAO, *Yearbook of Fishery Statistics: Catches and Landings* (Rome: 1992).
8. John Barham, "Argentina Ready to Bite at EC Fishing Deal," *Financial Times*, October 7, 1992.
9. FAO, "Aquaculture Production 1984–1990," *FAO Fisheries Circular No. 815 Revision 4*, Rome, June 1992.
10. Tim Coone, "Salmon Farms Blamed for Parasite Problem," *Financial Times*, August 6, 1992.
11. Caroline E. Mayer, "Caught Up in a Salmon Rivalry," *Washington Post*, April 24, 1991; James Buxton, " 'Cowboy' Salmon Farmers Come Under Fire," *Financial Times*, January 30, 1991.
12. "Salmon Farming Industry Booming in Chile," *Journal of Commerce*, September 29, 1992.
13. Larry Luxner, "Central American Export Tide Turns As Nations Cash In on Aquaculture," *Journal of Commerce*, May 28, 1992.
14. Robert Walters, "Aquaculture Catches On," *Mt. Vernon Register News*, July 31, 1987; conversion ratio for grain to beef based on Allen Baker, Feed Situation and Outlook staff, ERS, USDA, Washington, D.C., private communication, April 27, 1992; pork data from Leland Southard, Livestock and Poultry Situation and Outlook staff, ERS, USDA, Washington, D.C., private communication, April 27, 1992; feed-to-poultry conversion ratio derived from data in Robert V. Bishop et al., *The World Poultry Market— Government Intervention and Multilateral Policy Reform* (Washington, D.C.: USDA, 1990); poultry data from Linda Bailey, Livestock and Poultry Situation staff, ERS, USDA, Washington,D.C., private communication, April 27, 1992, and from various issues of *Feedstuffs*.

LITERACY GAINING SLOWLY

1. Based on 1.73 billion increase in adult literate population between 1950 and 1990, from United Nations Educational, Scientific and Cultural Organization (UNESCO), *International Yearbook on Education, Vol. XLII-1990, Literacy and Illiteracy in the World: Situation, Trends, and Prospects* (Paris: 1990).
2. Ibid.
3. United Nations, Statistical Division, *Compendium of Statistics on Illiteracy—1990 Edition* (Paris: UNESCO, 1990).
4. Ibid.
5. Author's estimate based on population data and projections from United Nations, *World Population Prospects 1990* (New York: 1991).
6. About 40 percent of the world's population of 3.1 billion, or more than 1.2 billion, were illiterate in 1962. By 1992, the percentage of illiterates had dropped to 25 percent, but with population up to about 5.5 billion, the absolute number of illiterates had increased to about 1.4 billion.
7. United Nations, Statistical Division, *Basic Education and Literacy* (New York: 1990).
8. The decline in number of adult illiterates from 1985 to 1990 averaged 480,000 people—just three one-hundredths of 1 percent of the total—per year.
9. United Nations, op. cit. note 3.
10. Ibid.
11. Ibid.
12. Jodi L. Jacobson, *Gender Bias: Roadblock to Sustainable Development*, Worldwatch Paper 110 (Washington, D.C.: Worldwatch Institute, September 1992).
13. "Literacy as a Yardstick of Social Health," *Down to Earth*, November 15, 1992.
14. United Nations Development Programme (UNDP), *Human Development Report 1992* (New York: Oxford University Press, 1992).
15. Ibid.
16. G. Carron and Anil Bordia, eds., *Issues in Planning and Implementing National Literacy Programmes* (Paris: UNESCO, International Institute for Educational Planning, 1985).
17. UNDP, op. cit. note 14.
18. Ibid.
19. Ibid.
20. Shapour Rassekh, *Perspectives on Literacy: a Selected World Bibliography* (Paris: UNESCO, 1991).
21. UNDP, op. cit. note 14.

FERTILITY RATE DECLINE STALLS

1. Shiro Horiuchi, "Stagnation in the Decline of the World Population Growth Rate During the 1980s," *Science*, August 7, 1992.
2. Ibid.
3. Ibid.
4. Population Reference Bureau (PRB), *1993 World Population Data Sheet* (Washington, D.C.: 1993).
5. Horiuchi, op. cit. note 1.
6. Doubling times from PRB, op. cit. note 4.
7. Hirouchi, op. cit. note 1.
8. Ibid.
9. Ibid.
10. United Nations, Department of International Economic and Social Affairs, *Long-range World Popula-*

tion Projections: Two Centuries of Population Growth, 1950–2150 (New York: 1992).

11. Steven W. Sinding, The Rockefeller Foundation, "Getting to Replacement: Bridging the Gap Between Individual Rights and Demographic Goals," presented at IPPF Family Planning Congress, Delhi, India, October 23–25, 1992; figure of 10 is a revision given in Steven W. Sinding, The Rockefeller Foundation, remarks delivered at panel on "Population Policies for the 1990s and Beyond—From Rio to Cairo," International Development Conference, Washington, D.C., January 11, 1993.

12. Sinding, "Getting to Replacement," op. cit. note 11.

NUCLEAR ARSENAL DECLINE ON HOLD

1. Richard Fieldhouse et al., "Nuclear Weapon Developments and Unilateral Reduction Initiatives," in Stockholm International Peace Research Institute (SIPRI), *SIPRI Yearbook 1992: World Armaments and Disarmament* (Oxford: Oxford University Press, 1992); Elaine Sciolino, "U.S. and Russia Agree on Atomic-Arms Pact Slashing Arsenals and the Risk of Attack," *New York Times*, December 30, 1992; Serge Schmemann, "Bush and Yeltsin Sign Pact Making Deep Missile Cuts," *New York Times*, January 4, 1993. Including nonstrategic nuclear weapons, approximately 20,000 warheads will be left worldwide by 2003. The United Kingdom and France are planning to expand their arsenals, and cuts in the Chinese stockpile are unlikely. See "Nuclear Weapons After the Cold War: Too Many, Too Costly, Too Dangerous," *The Defense Monitor*, Vol. 22, No. 1, 1993.

2. Michael Renner, "Nuclear Arsenals Shrinking," in Lester R. Brown, Christopher Flavin, and Hal Kane, *Vital Signs 1992* (New York: W.W. Norton and Company, 1992).

3. William M. Arkin and Robert S. Norris, "Tiny Nukes for Mini Minds," *Bulletin of the Atomic Scientists*, April 1992; William M. Arkin, "Little Nuclear Secrets," *New York Times*, September 9, 1992; Tom A. Zamora, "New Jobs for Old Labs?," *Bulletin of the Atomic Scientists*, November 1992; Peter Grier, "Cold War Over, But U.S. Continues Designing New Nuclear Weapons," *Christian Science Monitor*, July 24, 1992.

4. Graham Allison et al. (eds.), *Cooperative Denuclearization. From Pledges to Deeds* (Cambridge, Mass.: Harvard University, John F. Kennedy School of Government, 1993).

5. Barbara Crossette, "4 Ex-Soviet States and U.S. in Accord on 1991 Arms Pact," *New York Times*, May 24, 1992; "Belarus Approves First Arms-Limitation Pact," *New York Times*, February 5, 1993.

6. Elaine Sciolino, "Russian Chaos Stalls Disarmament, Senate is Told," *New York Times*, March 10, 1993.

7. Allison et al., op. cit. note 4.

8. Don Oberdorfer, "Bush Offers $175 Million for Nonnuclear Ukraine," *Washington Post*, December 10, 1992.

9. Celestine Bohlen, "Ukraine, Stumbling Block at End of Nuclear Race," *New York Times*, January 1, 1993; Steven Erlanger, "Yeltsin Offers Guarantees if Kiev Backs Arms Pact," *New York Times*, January 16, 1993.

10. Erlanger, op. cit. note 9.

11. Bohdan Pyskir, "Ukraine Needs Reassurance from West," *New York Times*, January 21, 1993; Oleh Bilorus, "Ukraine Needs Protection," *New York Times*, February 11, 1993.

12. Chrystia Freeland, "Ukraine Having Second Thoughts About Giving Up Nuclear Weapons," *Washington Post*, November 6, 1992; Serge Schmemann, "Ukraine Finds Nuclear Arms Bring a Measure of Respect," *New York Times*, January 7, 1993.

13. START I treaty provisions from Regina Cowen Karp, "The START Treaty and the Future of Strategic Nuclear Arms Control; Appendix 1A: Excerpts from the 1991 START Treaty and Related Documents," in SIPRI, op. cit. note 1; START II from "Treaty Between the United States of America and the Russian Federation on Further Reduction and Limitation of Strategic Offensive Arms," Official Text, as provided by U.S. Arms Control and Disarmament Agency, Washington, D.C., January 3, 1993; Russian reluctance from Sciolino, op. cit. note 6.

14. C.H. Bloomster et al., "Options and Regulatory Issues Related to Disposition of Fissile Materials from Arms Reduction," Pacific Northwest Laboratory, Richland, Wash., December 1990, prepared for the U.S. Department of Energy, presented at the Annual Meeting of the American Association for the Advancement of Science, Washington, D.C., February 18, 1991.

U.N. PEACEKEEPING SURGES

1. De Cuéllar quoted in Paul Lewis, "U.N. Chief Warns of Costs of Peace," *New York Times*, December 11, 1988.

2. William J. Durch and Barry M. Blechman, *Keeping the Peace: The United Nations in the Emerging World Order* (Washington, D.C.: The Henry L. Stimson Center, 1992).

3. Ibid.; Marjorie Ann Brown, "United Nations Peace-

keeping: Historical Overview and Current Issues,'' *CRS Report for Congress,* Congressional Research Service, Washington, D.C., January 31, 1990; Jeff Laurenti, *The Common Defense: Peace and Security in a Changing World* (New York: United Nations Association of the United States, 1992); United Nations Department for Public Information, private communications; numerous news clips.

4. Past U.N. spending from Durch and Blechman, op. cit. note 2; 1992 spending from Lucia Mouat, ''UN Grapples with Cost of Expanding Peace Role,'' *Christian Science Monitor,* May 18, 1992; 1993 estimate from Michael Littlejohns, ''Peace Cost Put at $1.55 bn,'' *Financial Times,* March 16, 1993.

5. 1990 and 1992 strength of peacekeepers from Lewis, op. cit. note 1, and from Lucia Mouat, ''UN Peacekeepers Face Tough, New Challenges,'' *Christian Science Monitor,* March 25, 1992.

6. If the warring parties in Bosnia accept a peace plan, the number of peacekeepers there could rise from the current 8,000 to 50,000 or more; Michael R. Gordon, ''U.S. Is Urging Nato to Prepare Force for Duty in Bosnia,'' *New York Times,* March 11, 1993. In Somalia, a 31,000-strong U.N. force is to be deployed by May 1993; ''U.N. Chief Sees Somalia Force Shifting in May,'' *New York Times,* March 4, 1993.

7. Number of countries from Brown, op. cit. note 3; cumulative number of peacekeepers from Boutros Boutros-Ghali, *An Agenda for Peace. Preventive Diplomacy, Peacemaking and Peace-keeping,* Report of the Secretary-General Pursuant to the Statement Adopted by the Summit Meeting of the Security Council on January 31, 1992 (New York: United Nations, 1992).

8. Durch and Blechman, op. cit. note 2.

9. For further discussion, see Indar Jit Rikhye, *Strengthening UN Peacekeeping: New Challenges and Proposals* (Washington, D.C.: United States Institute for Peace, 1992), and Laurenti, op. cit. note 3.

10. These issues are explored in David J. Scheffer et al., *Three Views on the Issue of Humanitarian Intervention* (Washington, D.C.: United States Institute of Peace, 1992).

11. Calculated from ''Status of Contributions as at December 31, 1992,'' United Nations Secretariat, New York, January 5, 1993.

12. For example, among the governments providing forces for the U.N. in Bosnia, those of Ukraine and Egypt have indicated a strong intention to pull out their contingents due to the increased danger and confused mandate; Hella Pick, ''Knee-Deep in the Imbroglio,'' (London) *Guardian,* September 11, 1992.

THE VITAL SIGNS SERIES

Some topics are included each year in Vital Signs; others, particularly those in Part Two, are included only in certain years. The following is a list of the topics covered thus far in the series, with the year or years each appeared indicated in parentheses. Plans are being made to make the data base available on diskette in the near future.

Part One: KEY INDICATORS

FOOD TRENDS
Grain Production (1992, 1993)
Soybean Harvest (1992, 1993)
Meat Production (1992, 1993)
Fish Catch (1992, 1993)
Grain Stocks (1992, 1993)
Grain Used for Feed (1993)

AGRICULTURAL RESOURCE TRENDS
Grain Area (1992, 1993)
Fertilizer Use (1992, 1993)
Irrigation (1992)

ENERGY TRENDS
Oil Production (1992, 1993)
Wind Power (1992, 1993)
Nuclear Power (1992, 1993)
Solar Cell Production (1992, 1993)
Natural Gas (1992)
Energy Efficiency (1992)
Geothermal Power (1993)
Coal Use (1993)
Hydroelectric Power (1993)

Carbon Efficiency (1993)
Compact Fluorescent Lamps (1993)

ATMOSPHERIC TRENDS
CFC Production (1992, 1993)
Global Temperature (1992, 1993)
Carbon Emissions (1992)

ECONOMIC TRENDS
Global Economy (1992, 1993)
Third World Debt (1992, 1993)
International Trade (1993)
Steel Production (1993)
Paper Production (1993)
Advertising Expeditures (1993)

TRANSPORTATION TRENDS
Bicycle Production (1992, 1993)
Automobile Production (1992, 1993)
Air Travel (1993)

SOCIAL TRENDS
Population Growth (1992, 1993)

Part Two: SPECIAL FEATURES